Caye Caulker

About the Book and Author

In the last decade, the island of Caye Caulker was transformed from a subsistence fishing village into an affluent enclave within a poor Caribbean country. This ethnographic study of the island recounts the economic success story of Caye Caulker, attributing the island's relative prosperity to several key features: the reorganization of the lobster fishing industry into producer cooperatives, the limiting and controlling of tourism, and the maintenance of sociocultural institutions that historically have created strong family networks and encouraged autonomy and self-sufficiency. Dr. Sutherland's unusual case study of positive development without external assistance makes a valuable contribution to our understanding of Third World development in general and local development in particular.

Anne Sutherland is associate professor of anthropology at Macalester College.

Caye Caulker

Economic Success in a
Belizean Fishing Village

Anne Sutherland

Westview Press / Boulder and London

Westview Special Studies in Social, Political, and Economic Development

This Westview softcover edition is printed on acid-free paper and bound in softcovers that carry the highest rating of the National Association of State Textbook Administrators, in consultation with the Association of American Publishers and the Book Manufacturers' Institute.

Published in 1986 in the United States of America by Westview Press, Inc.; Frederick A. Praeger, Publisher; 5500 Central Avenue, Boulder, Colorado 80301

Library of Congress Catalog Card Number: 86-50946
ISBN: 0-8133-7283-6

Composition for this book was provided by the author.
This book was produced without formal editing by the publisher.

Printed and bound in the United States of America

 The paper used in this publication meets the requirements of the American National Standard for Permanence of Paper for Printed Library Materials Z39.48-1984.

6   5   4   3   2   1

To Lois Hartley Sutherland
and Charles, Frankie and Benjamin Louis

Contents

Chapter I: INTRODUCTION

Chapter II: LOBSTER FISHING AND FISHERMEN

Chapter III: THE NORTHERN FISHERMEN COOPERATIVE
SOCIETY (with Laurie Kroshus)

Chapter IV: KINSHIP AND FAMILY STRUCTURE

Illustrations

TABLES

FIGURES

xii

MAPS

Preface

In the summer of 1972, to escape the unrelenting heat of Northern Belize where I was heading an anthropological expedition, I got into a sweaty cargo barge, inappropriately named 'The Mermaid', and chugged out to a small island called Caye Caulker that lies off the coast of Belize. As I stepped off the boat onto the back pier, mosquitoes landed on my arm in such numbers I could brush them off like bread crumbs on a table. I walked from the back pier past a shed where a generator alternately throbbed and clanked, on past the town garbage dump festering in a mangrove swamp, and entered a small village with two sand lanes of wooden plank houses on stilts. As I moved towards the windward side of the island, the warm Caribbean breeze became stronger, the numbers of mosquitoes thinned out, and I could see the waves breaking on the reef less than a mile out to sea. The sun beat on my head through a clear blue sky. The only sounds were those of the water lapping against piers poking out into the water, the soothing breeze rustling through the coconut fronds, and an occasional pelican splash landing in the water. People padded by silently with bare feet on soft sand, nodded disinterestedly, and went on about their business.

Caye Caulker felt like total isolation. Here was a fishing village whose only contact with the mainland of Belize was by boat, often a whole day's trip by sail or several hours twice a week on the Mermaid. There was no telephone on the island, hence no rapid way to contact the rest of the world. Visitors were obviously rare since there were no hotels. I spent the night on the veranda of a vacant house, and in the morning I searched the island for a place to buy a meal. In sheer desperation, I found Annette, one of a handful of resident Americans on the island, who made me a cup of coffee and scrambled eggs in exchange for news from abroad.

She also told me the local behavioral rule of thumb. "Whatever you do, people won't interfere. They're very tolerant except when you try to tell them what to do." Later, I discovered what she meant. When Clayton Adams was robbed of an expensive skiff motor for the sixth time in one year, he decided he would have to store the motor under his house instead of leaving it on the boat. Even though he knew the identity of the thief for at least some of the robberies, he shrugged it off with the comment, "He probably needed the money more than I do." Reluctant to interfere with each other, they are tolerant of foreign visitors as well.

Since 1972, I have visited Caye Caulker regularly, but in 1982 I decided to take a serious interest in the island. Even in 1982 Caye Caulker was a village that to the naked eye appeared poor, isolated, and undeveloped. The houses, still square wooden plank structures on stilts, were peeling and weathered. Everyone walked around barefooted and wore faded well-worn clothing. There was now one telephone line (with many extensions). News from the outside as well as messages from relatives and friends in other parts of the country came over the single radio station, Radio Belize.

These appearances were and still are totally misleading. The peeling paint, the worn clothes and the bare feet, all reasonable results of the Caribbean trade winds and sandy lanes, belie the real conditions on Caye Caulker. In less than ten years Caye Caulker has become one of the wealthier communities in Central America. Furthermore, the wealth is distributed among all big island families, and the island's culture and social organization have emerged from sudden wealth without major upheaval. In spite of an influx of major consumer goods such as refrigerators, gas stoves, washing machines, fast skiffs, and big boat motors, major services such as electricity and plumbing, and contact with several hundred tourists a year from all continents, Caye Caulker looks nearly the same as it did on my first visit twelve years before.

What happened during the intervening years is a case study in success. It is the success of a group of fishermen who, through a locally organized and controlled

fishing co-operative, have turned their efforts into a
lucrative fishing business. Their success is not merely
financial, it is also cultural. The combination of
cultural compatability and economic development is a story
worth telling.

This book is based on the research of a variety of
people using diverse methods under many different
conditions. It is a co-operative work in many ways. Over
a span of twelve years, I have observed Caye Caulker, and
Belize in general, on numerous visits. During this time,
I led four field trips to the island of approximately one
month duration, accompanied by undergraduate students from
Macalester College in June 1983 (six students), January
1983 (ten students), January 1984 (ten students) and
January 1985 (twenty-one students). All of these students
wrote research papers as part of the larger project. In
addition to my own participant observation during these
field trips and the work of these students, I have
benefited from the observations and stories of my mother,
who lived on the island between 1973 and 1977 as a member
of an island kin group through her marriage to an
islander. In conversation and through her numerous
letters she has added valuable information and insights to
this project. The data for this book therefore comes from
three sources: 1) my own participant observation over
twelve years, 2) the participant observation of my mother
living as another member of the community and 3) the
student projects undertaken during four formal field
trips. Among these students, the most valuable
contribution has come from Laurie Kroshus who participated
in two of the field trips and has worked with me closely
in writing up the results. She is largely responsible for
Chapter III on the social history of the Co-op. She has
also contributed to sections of Chapters VI and VIII.

It is apparent that such diverse sources also contain
diverse methods and kinds of data. There is the very
personal information and viewpoint of my mother whose main
interest was to understand her own new home and adapt to
it as a participant of the culture. There is the field
data of undergraduate research assistants, all of whom had
previous training in ethnographic methods of participant
observation and interviewing, following the James
Spradley[1] approach. Finally there is my own field work,
synthesis, and interpretation of all incoming data.

Although I have observed and interviewed the people
of Caye Caulker and participated in their daily lives
using traditional anthropological methods, I have also

tried as much as possible to adapt my field methods to the culture. My approach is to undertake field work in a way that is compatible with the people from whom I seek information. During field work with the Gypsies of California, for example, I found that direct questions were problematical to the Gypsies because they themselves rarely used the question-answer method to obtain reliable information. A direct question, among the Gypsies, generally provoked a misleading answer. On Caye Caulker, islanders learn information about each other by 'flapping around' or socializing informally. I have tried to gather information in much the same way. At the same time, I wanted to learn what the islanders think is important about themselves and to listen to the subjects that arouse their interest. Like Malinowski who wrote about the kula because the Trobrianders seemed to find it fascinating, I have written about topics such as fishing, kin groups, sexuality, tourism, and the fishing Co-operative, because these were the topics that emerged in conversation while flapping around. I am grateful to all the islanders, too numerous to mention individually, who have helped me in this endeavor.[2]

Furthermore, I am indebted to my colleagues Jack Weatherford, David McCurdy, Anna Meigs, and James Stewart for their encouragement and support. Jack Weatherford in particular has offered valuable advice in the preparation and focus of this manuscript. I am also grateful to James Gregory for his suggestions for improvement and his support for this work. His own work in Belize is a pioneering effort and has been very useful.

Many students contributed to this project. Among them I wish to thank Joy Barbre, Deborah Brady, Edward Booth, Matthew Cotton, Nick Edwards, Patricia Feely, Janet Fuller, Lisa Henderson, Sarah Hopkins, Ernest Lotito, Randi Lyders, Sally Mering, Betsy Rosen, Anne Schaefer, Eric Vacarella and Peter Woolen. Steven Frenkel was particularly helpful by mapping the households on the island.

Finally to Macalaster College I am grateful for allowing me to combine teaching and research through my ethnographic research interim course in Belize. To the Bush Foundation I am grateful for a faculty development grant that allowed me to make a field trip to Belize in 1982 to set up the interim research course. To Barbara Lankes, Charles Norman and Jackie Johnson I am grateful for their editorial help.

To Charles, Frankie, and Benjamin Louis I am grateful for their companionship and love during fieldwork with me and understanding while away.

Anne Sutherland

NOTES

[1]Spradley, James Participant Observation, Holt, Rinehart and Winston, 1980, and The Ethnographic Interview, Holt, Rinehart and Winston, 1979.

[2]The names of the islanders have been changed except for historical figures or political figures.

I

Introduction

Belize, a British colony until September, 1981, is a newly formed nation. As a relatively stable, democratic country in a politically volatile region, Belize now has great strategic importance to the United States. Located on the Central American mainland facing the Caribbean, Belize has physical and cultural ties to both regions (Map 1). Belize shares borders with Mexico and Guatemala and has long been involved in a still unresolved sovereignty dispute with Guatemala. Because of this dispute, British troops remain stationed in Belize today. The current political turmoil in Central America is also affecting Belize which has received a sudden increase in U.S. aid and a flow of refugees from Guatemala, El Salvador and Honduras.

The American government has targeted both the Caribbean basin and Central America as areas for major investment and political concern. U.S. policy in the region is to promote pro-American governments and discourage the creation of 'socialist' governments. The invasion of Grenada in 1983 and the political, economic and military involvement of the U.S. in Guatemala, El Salvador, Honduras and with Nicaraguan contras are only the most recent indications in a long history of U.S. moves in the region. In the last year and a half, the U.S. consulate in Belize has increased its personnel from five to 37 people, and through AID programs, $14 million is being invested in the country this year. The recent election of the UDP (United Democratic Party) after 30 years of PUP (People's United Party) government is viewed

2

Map 1

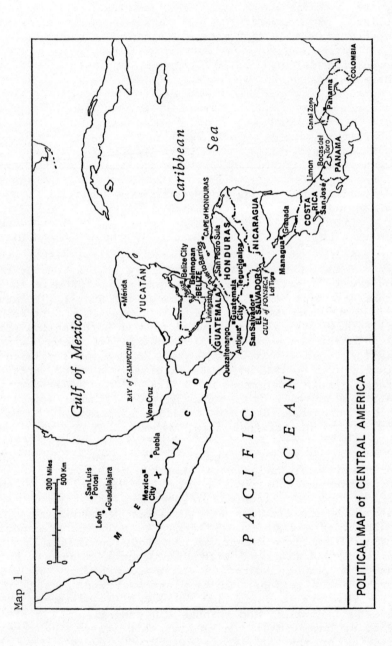

POLITICAL MAP of CENTRAL AMERICA

by American officials as a move to the 'right' that will create a favorable climate for American businesses in Belize[1]. Furthermore, the U.S. considers Belize a stable, democratic country with a pro-American government.

Belize has serious economic problems. Agricultural production is insufficient to feed the population, and there is virtually no industry. When a colony, Belize exported a few raw materials such as mahogany, logwood, chicle and later sugar cane, and it has always imported most of its consumer goods, including, to this day, twenty-five percent of all food. In short, Belize is a poor and dependent underdeveloped country[2]. Private U.S. business investments and economic assistance are suddenly increasing ostensibly to improve the economic situation in Belize and head off the development of a socialist form of government or political ties with Cuba.

This portrait of Belize raises a number of questions not only for the United States but for the Caribbean Basin as a whole. Given the situation of poverty and dependence, is there any alternative to the two regional choices of U.S. aid or socialism? If so, what are these alternatives? In such a position of dependency, why do some communities and regions achieve economic success while others remain poor?[3] Although dependency is a sad political reality, it is clear that people in the third world are faced daily with a variety of circumstances and a range of strategies to deal with those circumstances. Within the wider structure of underdevelopment, there remains the more specific question of what particular people do in particular circumstances and how they perceive their choices within their social environment.

This study of Caye Caulker, a small fishing community situated on an island just off the coast of Belize, will answer these questions. It demonstrates how this community in the Central American/Caribbean region has succeeded economically without becoming dependent on foreign aid and without a socialist political philosophy. Caye Caulker is an example of small-scale local development. The people of Caye Caulker have developed highly effective institutions and strategies to deal with production and marketing. Though I believe that key features of the Caye Caulker approach to local development could be applied to other underdeveloped countries, this is not an economic study. It is a holistic anthropological approach to the economic and cultural reasons for the development of one particular island in the Caribbean. A holistic anthropological approach emphasizes the connections between historical, cultural, and economic features without necessarily giving a priori importance to any one area of development. For this reason, above all, this study focuses on the specific case study rather than taking a comparative approach.

The development of Caye Caulker as an affluent enclave in a poor country can be attributed to several key features. First, a group of organized producers, lobster fisherman, deal directly with buyers from the international market who are competing with one another. The producers, acting together as a cooperative, negotiate as advantageous a price as demand allows without loss to middlemen and without the exploitative control of a monopolistic export company.

Second, the islanders have developed in ways that are compatible with their sociocultural institutions and values and draw on the strengths of those cultural features. Strong nuclear family ties combined with tolerance of individual differences, for example, encourage strong support networks of extended family members. Many of these institutions and ideals arise from general historical circumstances: a long history of colonial government, isolation from colonial political centers, and the relatively recent population of the island by refugees from the Caste Wars of Yucatan. Other institutions are responses to specific situations, such as economic exploitation by foreign companies. These historical and cultural circumstances have all helped to create a tradition of autonomy, individualism, and self-sufficiency.

Third, the islanders try to develop flexibility by balancing one area of endeavor with another. Within the range of available resources, the people have kept open as many options as possible. At the moment they supplement lobster production with tourism. They are fortunate to have rich lobster beds, but this environment is only lucrative to the islanders because they have kept control of production and markets. The pattern of local control in the fishing business is being repeated in the development of tourism.

The flexibility of the islanders' economic system can be linked to the flexibility of their sociocultural system. Both have a history of balancing a number of features. Located on the geographic and cultural boundary of the Latin American mainland and the Caribbean, the people of Caye Caulker have developed a combination of cultural features drawn from both areas. For example, they

combine Latin American patterns of household and family
structure with Caribbean patterns of sexual mores and
conjugal ties.

Arembepe: A Parallel Case

    The significance of Caye Caulker as a success story
can be highlighted by looking at the development of
parallel cases - kin-based fishing villages that have had
to deal with changing technology and marketing
opportunities. Arembepe, a fishing community on the
Northeast coast of Brazil, in a number of ways parallels
the development of Caye Caulker. In certain important
aspects, however, it provides an example of stark contrast
in results.[4]
    Arembepe was in the 1960's a place with an 'open
economic hierarchy' where it was possible to rise from the
very bottom to the very top through ambition, hard work
and good business sense.[5] Furthermore, there was very
little that was collective, communal, governmental or even
political in Arembepe.[6] The people lived lives fairly
free from outside interference.[7] All of these
characteristics are also found on Caye Caulker.
Furthermore, like Caye Caulker, fishing in Arembepe
replaced coconut plantations, became 'modernized', and was
eventually supplemented with tourism which provided new
economic opportunities.
    Arembepe has had the benefit of an almost
inexhaustible nearby market (the city of Salvador) for its
fish and a favorable economic situation in that the price
of fish rose faster than the inflation rate. This
favorable economic situation contrasts to the inequitable
and unfavorable economic situation on Caye Caulker in its
pre-cooperative days when markets were far away and
controlled by foreign (Canadian and American), companies
who paid a very poor price for lobster and reaped a large
profit. In this sense, pre-Co-operative Caye Caulker was
more like most of the fishermen in the world who have
limited access to marketing and limited control over the
prices they received. For example, on Coqueiral, a
Brazilian fishing village studied by Forman, the mayor and
president of the local fishing guild conspired to block
any increase in price the fishermen received, and with no
market nearby, the fishermen were prohibited from
marketing it themselves.[8] Unlike Coqueiral, the situation
in Arembepe was an attractive one for fishermen. The most
desirable job within Arembepe was fishing. Within the

community, an egalitarian ethos was closely associated
with kin-based levelling mechanisms so that no one became
too wealthy in relation to anyone else. Due to its
geographical position and isolation, Arembepe maintained
autonomy from the political center of Brazil and was
generally outside the Brazilian class structure. Everyone
in Arembepe was lower class, but no patrons operated in
Arembepe to bring people into the larger class structure.
Gradually, during the seventies, marketing improved when
roads were paved and motorized vehicles replaced the
donkey and cart. The produce from Arembepe fishermen
could reach the markets faster and in better condition and
still meet the steady demand. Although the fishermen had
no control of prices, the market situation was nonetheless
favorable.

Like Caye Caulker, Arembepe is an egalitarian, kin-
based society. Social gradations were present in Arembepe
in the 1960's, but it was not a stratified society. The
most important distinction within the community was that
between captain-owners of boats and workers on the boats.
This situation had changed by 1980 when, as in the rest of
Brazil, the rich were getting richer and the poor much
poorer. The form this change took in the fishing industry
was the result of the fact that in real terms fishermen
were catching fewer fish per days' labor than they had
during the 1960's, while boat owners were getting ten
times their previous profits. Social mobility between
owner and worker also decreased. In 1980 it took 5,500
kilos of fish to buy a boat whereas in 1964 a man had only
to sell 400 kilos of fish to acquire enough capital to buy
a boat and become a boat owner rather than a worker on
another man's boat. Kottak concludes, "As a result of
their poverty and powerlessness, the people of Arembepe
... have been compelled by external forces to give up a
large part of their previous autonomy, egalitarianism and
peace of mind. Like a thousand other places, Arembepe has
grown increasingly dependent on, and vulnerable to, a
world political economy of which its inhabitants have
little understanding and over which they have even less
control."[9]

In this respect, Caye Caulker represents an exception
to the "thousand other places". Regardless of the many
parallels in development between Arembepe and Caye Caulker
- the motorization of the fishing industry, the
development of tourism as an alternative source of income,
the combination of egalitarian ideals, entrepreneurial
spirit and strong family ties, Caye Caulker has gone in a

different direction. The people of Caye Caulker organized politically, and they took control of production and marketing. In short, they achieved economic and political independence.

The Caribbean-Central American Region

Although the scholarly literature of both the Caribbean and Latin America is extensive and well-developed, there are very few major studies of Belize in any of the disciplines of the social sciences. Even in the popular press, Belize is unknown. Because it is a newly independent country, most people have not heard of Belize until reminded that it was formerly British Honduras.[10] In a preface to one of the few major published studies of Belize, Colonialism and Underdevelopment: Processes of Political Economic Change in British Honduras, by Norman Ashcraft, Lambros Comitas remarks,

> Because of its location, history, economy and the heterogeneity of its population, British Honduras has long been a rich but unused laboratory for the study of a variety of social science problems. Geographic isolation from the Antilles and the mainstream of West Indian research, and the physical difficulties of travel within the territory are factors which help to explain the paucity of systematic study of a territory which will soon achieve independence. The limited number of publications on British Honduras tends to be concentrated in archeology, particularly Mayan prehistory, on narrowly focused treatments of specific political and social institutions, on the legal issues surrounding boundary disputes with Guatemala and Honduras, and, not unexpectedly, on lumbering, the historically dominant economic activity of the territory . . . almost nothing of full size in social and cultural anthropology, economics, political science, and allied disciplines has yet appeared in print.[11]

According to Comitas, Belize has been neglected because it is part of the mainland of Central America, but as a former British colony, it is culturally, ethnically,

and politically more similar to the British West Indies.
This has resulted in isolation from mainstream West Indian
research while remaining a cultural and linguistic anomaly
to Latin America. The very reason for neglect, cultural
ambiguity, is also a reason for interest. Belize, in
general, presents an unusual cultural situation worthy of
study for a number of reasons.

First, Belize represents an exception to virtually
every pattern found in the rest of the Caribbean. In
recent comparative studies of the Caribbean region,[12]
Belize is dismissed as an 'exception' to the 'main
elements' of Caribbean history and economy, colonial
mercantilism and a slavery based plantation system of
rigid color-class hierarchies. Yet Belize also is
regarded as a Caribbean nation with a Creole (African and
European) culture, among other cultures, and has at least
some of the same developmental features of colonialism
found in other Caribbean societies. Detailed studies of
what this exception means for any particular situation are
still lacking.

Second, because the region is a political
backwater, a variety of cultural groups have flourished in
the absence of a strong central government. Caye Caulker,
for example, has a history of ignoring power hierarchies
outside its boundaries and guarding zealously its local
independence. Within this context of political autonomy,
Caye Caulker has also developed a society with relatively
little social hierarchy. The fishermen's cooperative,
with its egalitarian membership and local control of
production and distribution, is a reflection of the
society within which it developed.

Third, the region presents cultural features that
are an unusual combination of Latin American and Caribbean
patterns. On Caye Caulker, for example, Latin American
types of household and family structure prevail. Great
importance is given to relationships with cognatic kin who
perform important economic and social functions.
Households are based on a conjugal relationship and are
composed mainly of nuclear families. The importance of
cognatic kin and the prevalence of nuclear family
households contrast with the Caribbean family which
characteristically centers around the relationship of a
mother and children and does not typically contain a
nuclear family. On the other hand, on Caye Caulker the
rules and practices concerning sexual mores, conjugal
ties, and personal values are more characteristic of the
Caribbean rather than Latin America practices.

Belize

    Belize is a small nation that is both Central
American and Caribbean.[13] Bounded on the north and west
by Mexico and on the south and west by Guatemala, its
entire eastern boundary stretches along the Caribbean
coast. With a total of only 8,867 square miles, Belize is
the second smallest country on the American continent,
approximately 174 miles long and 68 miles wide.
    The Belizean mainland can be roughly divided into
two geographical areas (Map 2). The northern half of the
country is a fertile plain on a bed of limestone with a
low swampy coastline. Belize City itself is only 18
inches above sea level. This northern section was settled
earliest and developed primarily because of the navigable
rivers which provided the transportation necessary for the
logwood and lumber trades that flourished during the
period of settlement. In the southern half of the
country, the land rises rapidly from the low coastal plain
to the Maya Mountains which peak some twenty miles inland.
The Mayas, a very old chain of quartzite and granite
peaks, run roughly north-south and have few minerals and
generally poor soil. For these reasons and the lack of
transportation, the southern section developed much later
than the northern region.
    Ten to fifteen miles offshore lies a coral ridge
which extends the entire length of the coastline. Small
coral islands along this ridge, known as cayes, make up
212 square miles. There are three types of cayes in this
chain. Wet cayes are submerged at least part of the time
and can support only mangrove swamps. A second type,
equally uninhabitable, is the bare outcroppings of coral.
The third type are the sandy islands with coconut palms
and lush tropical undergrowth. The largest and best known
of the inhabitable cayes are in the northern part of the
chain of islands. Caye Caulker is one, along with
Ambergris Caye, St. George's Caye, and Caye Chapel.
    Outside of this chain of cayes is another coral
ridge just a few miles seaward, the barrier reef. It is
the second largest barrier reef in the world and stretches
190 miles in the crystal clear water along the coast.
This massive wall of coral, broken only by a few channels,
shelters the sandy islands from erosion by waves. While
much of the Great Barrier Reef of Australia is dead, the
Belizean reef is alive and relatively unpolluted. Coral
polyps still grow in large colonies that provide

Map 2

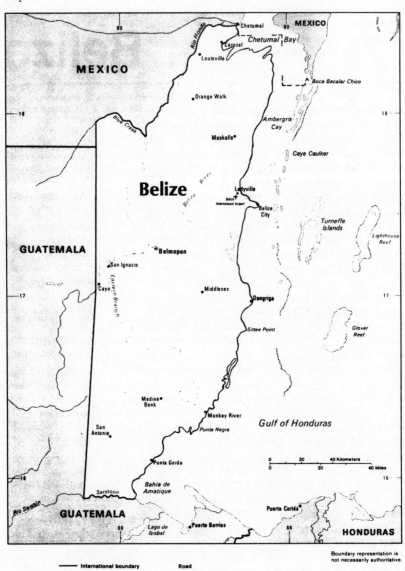

protection for numerous fish. Lobster and edible fish such as snapper, grouper, jack, and grunt feed in and around the reef. Rays, sharks and porpoises are also seen inside the reef. Beyond the reef is 'the blue' where the seabed drops from 15 feet through a series of plateaus to 4,000 feet. In the blue there are numerous larger game fish such as mackerel, kingfish, wahoo, tuna, sailfish, marlin, and barracuda.

Climate

The climate in Belize is subtropical with distinct wet and dry seasons. The dry season generally lasts from February to May and the wet season from June to January. The amount of precipitation varies considerably from North to South. Corozal in the north receives about 40 to 50 inches of rain per year while Punta Gorda in the south receives an average of 160 inches. Temperatures range from 50° to $95^{\circ}F$. in Belize City with an average yearly temperature of 80°. Trade winds off the Caribbean temper the humidity, which averages about 83%.

During the year, the easy flow of established weather patterns may be interrupted by one of several calamities. Belize is situated in the Hurricane Belt and has often been hit hard. Hurricanes have ravaged the coastal cities twenty-one times since 1787. Belize City itself was destroyed by hurricanes so many times that the government finally decided to move the capital 50 miles inland to Belmopan. Though the most severe damage is often restricted to a narrow swath of the hurricane's storm track, high winds, heavy rain and rough seas effect a much larger area.

During the winter months, December through February, severe storms called 'northers' sweep down from North America across the Gulf of Mexico, bringing with them rain and strong winds. These storms only last for a few days, but they interrupt fishing activity and influence mass movements of fish and lobster. Fishermen report an increase in their catch just before the arrival of a storm. These storms supply most of the drinking water and ground water on the cayes.

A third weather occurrence is the 'mauger' season. Usually occurring during August, the mauger season is an extremely dry, calm period when trade winds drop off for a week or more. In the hot stillness, insects become ferocious. Life on the cayes virtually halts until this period passes and the winds return. People close

Map 3

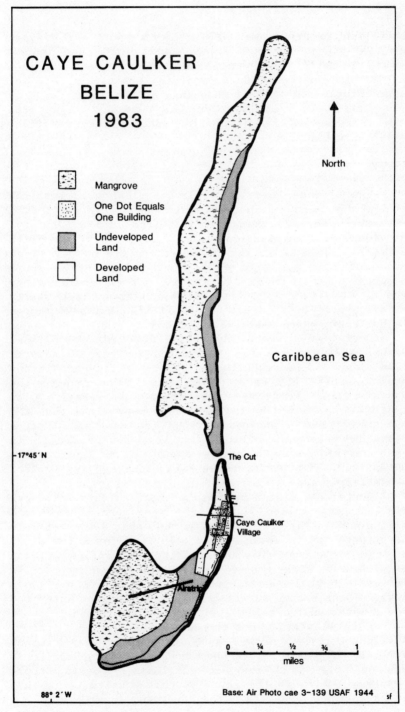

CAYE CAULKER
BELIZE
1983

Mangrove

One Dot Equals
One Building

Undeveloped
Land

Developed
Land

North

Caribbean Sea

-17°45′N

The Cut

Caye Caulker
Village

Airstrip

Caribbean Sea

0   ¼   ½   ¾   1
miles

88° 2′ W

Base: Air Photo cae 3-139 USAF 1944   sf

themselves in their houses and venture out only when it is absolutely necessary, flapping towels around their heads at the clouds of mosquitoes as they run.

Caye Caulker

Caye Caulker is an island situated 21 miles northeast of Belize City, 11 miles south of Ambergris Caye and one mile west of the barrier reef (Map 2). The only access to the island is by boat. Periodically, attempts to build an airstrip on the island take place, but it has never been completed. Both San Pedro and Caye Chapel have functioning airstrips. Until recently, The Mermaid made regular trips with cargo and passengers about three times a week, and the Coca Cola Company now has a regular supply run. For passengers, the main transportation is provided by islanders who run skiffs to and from Belize City. "Hershey," for example, goes to Belize City every day with about 12 passengers and charges U.S. $6.00 each way. During the height of the tourist season, from December to February, several boats run each day.

The island is four miles long, but the inhabited part includes an area less than a mile long, from the 'cut' at the northern end to the school building in the south. A few foreigners have built houses southwest of the school in a swampy area known as 'Marcialtown', but few islanders live at that end of the island. North of the cut is uninhabitable and consists mainly of mangrove swamps (Map 3).

The village consists of two main sand roads running north to south, cut by a number of cross roads. There is a main front pier in the middle of the village facing the reef and a main back pier where large boats dock. Located at the back pier are the Coca Cola and Belikan beer offices, the marina and cold rooms of the cooperative, and the generators for electricity on the island (Map 4).

The only cement public buildings are the police station, the community center, and the school. There are two policemen, a nurse, and several school teachers. The policemen and nurse are always nonislanders appointed by the government. The teachers are usually island women who have obtained their teacher's certificate in Belize City. The school, which operates on the British system, goes from Infant school through Standard Six. For a secondary education, young people from the island must go to a 'college' in Belize City.

Map 4

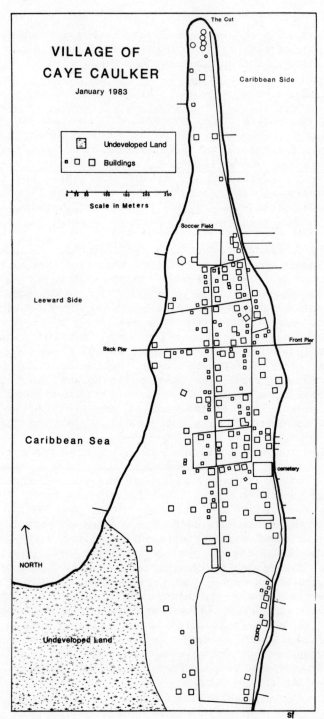

VILLAGE OF
CAYE CAULKER
January 1983

The Cut

Caribbean Side

Undeveloped Land

Buildings

Scale in Meters

Soccer Field

Leeward Side

Back Pier

Front Pier

Caribbean Sea

cemetery

NORTH

Undeveloped Land

Houses on the island are wooden frame structures with aluminum sheet roofing. Most houses are built high on posts to catch the sea breeze. Some of these houses have enclosed the open part under the house to make rooms for tourists or extra living space. These were the first hotels on the island. The aluminum roofs have gutters to catch the rain and channel it into a tank by the side of the house. Most houses also have wells. Well water is drinkable because the island is on a limestone escarpment, but it is mainly used for washing because of the slightly saline taste. In the dry season, rainwater becomes scarce.

Caye Caulker is a sandy island that will not support agricultural production. Coconut trees grow in abundance and papaya, lime, breadfruit, banana, plantain and coco fruit trees also thrive. In addition, herbs such as oregano and apozote can be grown. Flowering trees such as the hibiscus, geiger, and flamboyan, and tropical vegetation such as crotons, succulents, spider lilies, bougainvillea, and periwinkle are plentiful. The sand is cleared of weeds and vines wtih a machete, but they grow back very quickly.

Pelicans and frigate birds hunt along the coast for fish. Lizards, boa constrictors, and crabs (both hermit crabs and rock crabs) are native to the island. The insect population, locally referred to as 'flies,' is extremely vigorous due to the proximity of mangrove swamps. During the rainy season, from May to September, sand flies and mosquitoes are 'fierce,' as the islanders say, and all work may come to a halt on a bad day. Malaria and dengue fever cases have been known to occur.

Population and Language

According to Eduardo Lemos, a Justice of the Peace on Caye Caulker, a 1980 census reported 413 residents. There are approximately 100 houses and 175 children in school. People on Caye Caulker are ethnically designated as 'Spanish' and are of Yucatecan Mestizo descent. There has also been some intermarriage with Creoles, a mixture of African and European peoples. Because of the constant exposure to sun, people are dark-skinned with hair that is bleached blond at the ends.

There are three languages in general use on the island. English, the official language of Belize, is taught in school and is spoken by virtually all islanders. They also speak English Creole and Spanish. Most people can use all three languages with complete ease. A few of the older people still are most comfortable in Spanish.

NOTES

1.   Interview with Charles Jenkins, AID, American Consulate, Belize City.

2.   For example, see Malcolm Cross (1978), Norman Ashcraft (1973), and Edmund Gordon (1981).

3.   An example of a parallel study of a small Caribbean island is Island Adrift by Wout van den Bor (1981). Many of the same conditions exist--isolation from a political center, fishing and tourism, a lack of community solidarity, etc., but the result has been stagnation and poverty.

4.   Kottak, Conrad Phillip, Assault on Paradise, Social Change in a Brazilian Village, New York, Random House, 1983.

5.   Ibid, p. 81.

6.   Ibid, p. 60.

7.   Ibid, p. 78

8.   Forman, Shepard, The Raft Fishermen, Tradition and Change in the Brazilian Peasant Economy, Bloomington: Indiana University Press, 1970.

9.   Kottak, p. 3.

10.   A recent history of Belize was even titled Formerly British Honduras (Setzekorn, William, 1975). For more recent histories of Belize, see Bolland, O. Nigel The Formation of a Colonial Society, Johns Hopkins University Press, 1977; Kerns, Virginia, Women and the Ancestors, Univ. of Illinois Press, 1983.

11.   Ashcraft (1973), page v.

12.   See, for example, Gordon K. Lewis (1983) and Malcolm Cross (1979).

13.   The following information on the geography and climate of Belize (pages 6-9) comes from Setzekorn, William (1975), pages 3, 69-72.

II

Lobster Fishing and Fishermen

On Caye Caulker, fishing is the mode of production
that most affects the political economy and development of
the community. Fishing is both individualistic (at the
level of production) and collaborative (at the level of
marketing).   Thus it fosters and is supported by
individual entrepreneurship and a network of social ties.
The nature of fishing on Caye Caulker, the forms it takes,
and the social relationships developed around it, provide
the underpinnings of its most successful feature: the
formation of the fishermen's Co-operative that emerges
from the struggle with foreign monopolies.
Fishing is the major source of income and work for
men. Being a fisherman is a source of self-esteem as well
as a means of obtaining independence as an adult man who
can support a wife and children. In addition, there is an
intangible aspect to fishing that is both aesthetic and
emotional. Many men enjoy fishing and appear to experience
genuine pleasure when bringing in a good catch.   Most men
on Caye Caulker are fishermen; they derive personal
satisfaction as well as prestige from being good
fishermen.
Basically there are four kinds of fishing on Caye
Caulker: lobster traps, diving, line fishing, and fish
traps.[1]   Each type of fishing requires a different
technical knowledge of equipment and a slightly different
knowledge of marine life.   Those who work with lobster
traps must know where to set traps, how to build, weight,
and season the traps as well as haul, clean, and mark
traps. Divers must know where to find lobster at the reef

19

and how to use a hook or spear. Line fishing and fish
traps require knowledge of where and when schools of fish
are found and when the fish are running; typically these
decisions are determined by seasons and phases of the
moon. In addition, fishermen need to know the use of
lines and, for fish traps, how to construct and maintain a
trap. Most of the older fishermen have all of these
skills. Some of the younger ones possess only some of
them. For example, a young man may be a good diver but
may not have the experience or resources (credit for traps
and a territory) to work his own lobster traps. Many
learn the skills by working with relatives or by working
for large operations that go far from Caye Caulker to
areas such as the Turneffe Islands or Half Moon Caye.
Line fishing also seems to be most prevalent among older
men, but it is not as commercially profitable as lobster
and has not been passed on to many younger men. At the
present time, fish trap production is not very common
around Caye Caulker, probably because of the greater
profits possible with lobster. Fishermen from Sarteneja,
on the other hand, work mainly with fish traps that they
construct at the leeward side of the caye, in the Bay of
Chetumal, and along the northern coast of Ambergris Caye.
    In all cases, regardless of the method of
production, membership in the locally organized Northern
Fishermen Cooperative is essential for fishing to be
really profitable. The co-op provides market and handling
facilities, an immediate cash payment and a rebate at the
end of the fishing season, and credit for supplies during
the year. The Northern Fishermen Co-op gives the best
price for lobster and fish available in the whole country.
Because of this advantage, several fishermen from the
Carbena Co-op in San Pedro and the entire Sarteneja
Cooperative have joined the Northern Fishermen
Cooperative. Profit from fishing is a direct result of
the inception of the co-op, and is a major factor in the
prestige that men can now derive from fishing. As one man
put it,

> A few years ago people (in Belize) looked down
> on fishermen - until they started to make
> money. Now (fishermen) can sit with the bank
> manager. The old attitude is still around,
> but kids who come from the city and fish with
> their relatives to make spending money often
> make more than some people in Belize City make
> in a year.

Fishing, as a mode of production, is consistent with the Caye Caulker ideals of individualism and independence. In fact, it has been argued that independence is a 'psychoculturally adaptive characteristic of small-scale fishermen' and that in fishing communities organizations fail that do not take into account this psychological characteristic.[2] In fishing, as it is practiced on Caye Caulker, men work alone or as partners with one or two other men, often relatives. Individual men have control of their own production, which depends on their knowledge of the sea and of fishing technology as well as the support of their families. Most men do not have to work for others to make a living. Those who do work for others, to learn the trade or because they do not have the advantages of family support, are often paid according to a share of the catch. Larger fishing operations do form a hierarchy of employer (owner of the boat and materials) and workers, but even then all of these men work side by side, engaged in the same work.

Fishing is also compatible with family organization and loyalty. Men inherit lobster territories and acquire the knowledge they need from older male relatives, usually a father or uncle. Both knowledge and resources are thus passed on through families, and men from successful fishing families have advantages over others. The most expensive pieces of equipment are a skiff with a motor and lobster traps. These may be provided by a man's family or purchased with loans from the co-op. Because lobster territories near Caye Caulker are in the hands of islanders, lobster trap fishing is the most difficult to begin without family help. It is also the most profitable of all the forms of fishing.

Although some measure of control of resources is affected by the observance of a lobster season, all forms of fishing resemble a 'robber economy.' The sea contains a resource that is available to any individual who is willing to work it and can learn the skills necessary to make a living at it. Until that resource is depleted, every man is an entrepreneur who has access to the major economic resource of the island.

Access to the resources needed to get started as a lobster fisherman - a territory, boat, motor, traps and membership in the co-op are not equally available to everyone on the island. Men who learn a skill from a father or uncle, who become members of the co-op early in life by demonstrating their ability as a fisherman, and who inherit a good lobster territory have definite advantages and become wealthier than other men. These advantages do not create an elite with the absolute control of economic resources such as occurs in a plantation system where land is a limited resource under the absolute control of certain families and individuals. Fishing knowledge and new lobster territories, farther afield, are available to the industrious and enterprising fisherman. However, they do create status and economic differences among islanders, and between islanders and other Belizeans.

The Lobster

The Caribbean or spiny lobster (<u>Panulirus</u> <u>argus</u>) inhabits warm waters, has spines rather than claws for defense, and is part of the crayfish family. In taste and appearance it is much like the Northern American lobster (<u>Homarus</u> <u>americanus</u>) and is considered a gourmet treat by American and European diners who pay a high price for it.

Caye Caulker fishermen use two methods for harvesting lobster (or 'bugs' as they are sometimes called): diving and setting traps. Lobsters travel and feed at night and look for dark caves to hide in during the day. For this reason, the many crevices in the coral formations of the reef provide an ideal hiding place for lobster and an excellent hunting ground for a diver who knows where to look. The lobsters' daytime search for a safe, dark place is also put to use by the men who set traps. The traps, or 'pots' as they are sometimes called, are trapezoid-shaped slatted wood crates, approximately three and a half feet long and one and a half feet high. The trap has a hole with a wooden funnel at one end that the lobster can enter but cannot leave. Because the lobster is looking for a hiding place by day, fishermen do not put bait in the traps. In addition to traps, some men use large metal drums. These drums are pinched together at the top to prevent the lobster from escaping. Several holes punched along the sides and bottom allow water and sand to drain out so that when the fisherman pulls them up, they are not too heavy.

Lobster Trap Fishing

The most profitable fishing on Caye Caulker is done with lobster traps. Lobster traps produce a much higher yield over time and are less labor intensive than diving for lobster. However, the use of lobster traps requires a capital outlay to buy materials for traps, and the acquisition of a lobster territory. Since lobster territories are limited, islanders who belong to one of the island families usually begin by working with a relative and eventually establish a territory near that relative. Furthermore, a man may be able to get started in a territory with a small number of traps obtained through financial help from his family. When he produces enough to become a member of the co-op, he can increase the number of traps by using his credit with the co-op. Thus, islanders have a number of advantages over non-islanders in becoming lobster fishermen and men from families with good lobster territories have an advantage over men from families without territories.

Every year the fishermen set their traps in the same general area. Each fisherman has his own territory. These territories are not officially mapped and there are no recorded boundaries. Although it is difficult to know the location of every single territory, each man knows the location and boundaries of territories in the general vicinity of his own. The location of territories is fairly public knowledge, but the exact location of an individual man's traps is a carefully guarded secret.

Some territories are better than others, and a prized territory is one that 'fishes good' year after year. Territories vary in size depending on the amount of traps a man has and on whether he has been able to expand his holding. There are several ways to obtain a territory. The most common way is for a boy to inherit one from his father or another close relative, such as an uncle or cousin. For example, one man has had his territory for over twenty- five years. He obtained it from his cousin with whom he worked as a boy. After his cousin retired, it became his own, and he now works it alone. Another young man has a territory that originally belonged to his father. When he was fourteen, he set 15 to 20 of his own traps near his father's traps. A year later his father retired and gave him his territory. He now works this territory with his younger brother.

Acquiring a territory other than through inheritance from a relative is very difficult. Occasionally a man may

work with a nonrelative who has an established territory.
He may then have an opportunity to take over when the man
retires, or to start his own territory alongside his
partner's. It is possible to expand the size of a
territory in the same way. The strategy is to add a few
extra traps each season on the outer edge of the territory
and thus to ease slowly into new areas.

Still another way a fisherman may obtain a territory
involves setting a few traps on the edge of a friend's
territory. By adding a few more traps every season, a
fisherman may secure a particular area. But a fisherman
who attempts to set traps in an unclaimed area quickly
discovers that all the workable locations close to Caye
Caulker have been taken. Though it is possible to fish
far from the Caye, islanders claim that the extra time and
transportation costs make such ventures unprofitable.
Finally, a fisherman can buy a territory from another
islander who has no heirs or is willing to sell for some
other reason. The difficulties of acquiring a territory
are a contributing factor to the frequent theft that takes
place from lobster traps.

Setting Traps

Within his territory each fisherman must decide
exactly where to place his traps. Traps are never placed
at or very near the reef because the water is so rough it
would smash the traps on the rocks. Traps must be set far
enough from the reef to avoid damage and loss.

The seabed surrounding Caye Caulker contains
excellent lobster fishing but some areas fish better than
others. There are certain clues that indicate a good
fishing spot. For example, on the border between a grassy
area and a 'white spot' (sandy areas clear of vegetation),
banks form under the grass. Lobster are attracted to this
area because it provides a dark spot to hide. Another
good spot is where lobster come in from the 'blue' (the
open sea), at breaks in the reef. Traps closest to breaks
in the reef get more lobster than ones farther away.
Fishermen set traps in the same areas every year unless
they happen to 'fish bad' one year. If a fisherman sees
an area he thinks might be good, he will set ten to
twenty-five traps there to try it out. He never sets all
the traps in one area but tries to scatter them around the
best spots. An area that has proven itself will have the
most traps. Traps are generally placed no closer than one
hundred yards apart.

Figure I. Lobster Trap Setting Patterns

(by Eric Vacarella)

Diagrams a and b are earlier methods of setting traps. Both are located using the island land mark system explained in Figure II. Individual traps are located by their relative position to the marker poles. Such "straight line" methods have now been abandoned by many fishermen because these patters are too easy for thieves to locate. This third locating method (diagram c) uses a more random zigzag pattern at the same time using poles, not "sea marks as the primary location aids.

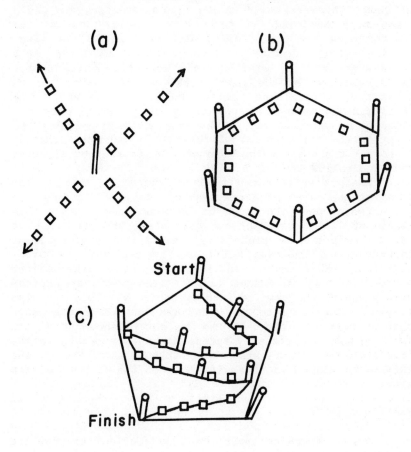

The established fishermen on Caye Caulker generally have between 150 and 500 traps and have to know the location of every one. In Florida, fishermen rope their traps together and mark them with a buoy. But the water around Caye Caulker is so shallow that if they were marked with a buoy, they would be too easily stolen. The fishermen employ several strategies to remember where their traps are and at the same time keep them hidden from others. First of all, they always set and check the traps in a given order. Second, they set the traps so that they form a pattern, often a zigzag pattern, which must be committed to memory. Each fisherman creates his own individual pattern which he keeps secret (See Figure I). In addition to the pattern, there are other memory aids. Traps can be located by establishing two points or landmarks which are used to triangulate the position of a given trap or group of traps. One point, called the running mark, is marked by a stick placed in the sand, jutting out of the water, or may be the leeward edge of a grass strip in the water or of a specific 'white spot.' The second, called the stop mark, may be the tip of an island, or a prominent tree or bush on an island. The fisherman approaches a spot using the running mark and lines it up with the stop mark using his boat as the third point in the triangle (See Figure II). Another strategy is to set traps along the edge of a white spot or a grassy spot and follow its curve.

Before setting new traps or returning them to the water at the start of a new season, they are put in a pen in the water near the shore to 'season' them. After this treatment, they are taken out, scrubbed, and are ready to set. They are then weighted with small chunks of coral or rocks so that they will not easily tip over or shift position. Where the current is strong, more rocks have to be put in than in calmer areas. The rocks are spread evenly inside the trap to insure stability. Then the trap is gently lowered into the water and watched to make sure that it remains upright on its descent to the bottom. In murky areas, a white polystyrene float is attached to the trap so that it floats about three feet beneath the surface. This makes it easier to spot the trap under the water.

Hauling Traps

Fishermen check their traps by sections every three to seven days. They will check an area often if 'the

Figure II. Locating a Lobster Territory

(by Eric Vacarella)

Territory is defined by a series of poles and is located relative to pre-determined island landmarks. Within the territory traps are located by the use of "sea marks" and their positions relative to the boundary poles.

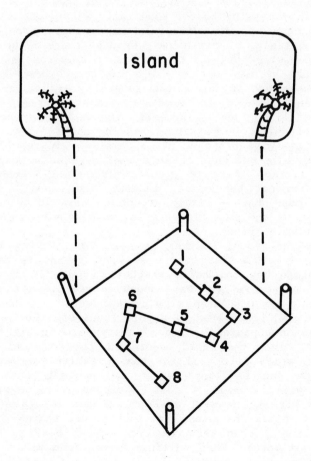

lobster are running good' or less frequently if they are not hauling in many lobster.

Some men work alone, others with a partner. In a partnership, usually the older man owns the territory and the second man or boy is a younger relative or friend. One man runs the motor and hauls the traps while the other stands on the bow of the skiff and looks for the traps. A partner also helps remove the lobster from the traps and throw them into an empty trap on board their skiff.

After arriving at the area where the traps are located, the first step is to line up the landmarks in order to find the traps. One common problem is that sometimes the sticks a man has put in the water have been broken off by passing boats, especially sugar barges. If this has happened, the fisherman must circle around to locate the remains of the stick. When he finds it he will put in a new stick or pole to serve as a temporary marker. Occasionally he may not be able to locate the broken stick, but since he knows the general location he can often calculate where his traps are without it.

After lining up the markers, the fisherman goes to the first trap in the pattern. Finding the first trap is often difficult as traps do not always stay in one place. A light wind, a current, or an animal such as a porpoise may move a trap. Also if a thief has pulled a trap, it probably has not been reset in the right spot. So a fisherman may have to circle around an area to spot the first trap, at the same time keeping in mind wind patterns and current directions.

Calm and sunny weather is best for hauling traps because they are easier to spot. When a trap is found, the fisherman has to decide whether to pull it or not. The water is generally clear enough to see it sitting on the bottom. When a trap sits in the water for several days, the wood is covered by a thin layer of silt, making it whitish in appearance. When lobster are in the trap, they crawl along the inside searching for an escape and remove the white silt. If the trap is white, no lobster are inside and as long as it is properly set, the fisherman will leave it. If it is tipped over, no matter what color it is, he will pull it and set it again. If the trap is black, he knows that lobster are inside.

Pulling a trap requires great upper body strength and is hard work. When pulling traps, some men wear a support to prevent hernias. One fisherman claims that if a trap is full of lobster it weighs less, or seems to weigh less because it 'gives you courage to pull it up.'

A trap is pulled with a 25-foot long pole that has a metal hook on the end. Keeping his back straight and his knees bent, the fisherman pulls the heavy trap. When it reaches the surface, he grabs it with one hand, using the other to set the pole on board. He must use both hands to lift it onto a special board nailed on the rim of the boat. It is then placed on a small canvas on the floor of the boat. The canvas helps collect debris and keeps the skiff cleaner. Once the trap is on board, the fisherman removes the lid and grabs the lobster by the antennae, tossing it into a container (usually an empty pot). Undersize lobster (less than four ounces) are thrown back into the water because they cannot be sold to the co-op.

A small piece of canvas is placed over the container with lobster to protect them from the sunlight that will otherwise cause them to spoil quickly. Mud and growth are brushed off the trap, the rocks are distributed evenly, and it is reset in the same spot. To do this the fisherman must know exactly how far he has drifted and motor back to the right spot. Finally, the canvas on the floor is rinsed in the water and any debris in the bottom of the skiff is wiped up, and the fisherman can motor to the next trap.

There are a few variations from this procedure when hauling a metal drum. When a drum is spotted, the fisherman first checks to see if any antennae are sticking out of the entrance. To do this, he uses a glass bottomed box that allows him to see the drum very clearly. These boxes were used by divers before masks were introduced to the island. Because drums are very heavy, most fisherman haul a drum only if they see antennae. A drum is pulled using the same technique as for a trap except that the drum must be drained while it rests on the rim of the boat. If the bottom of the drum is rusted, it will be repaired on the spot by inserting a bottom taken from another drum into the old drum and pounding it into place. Some fishermen do not replace a rusted bottom but will dive to a damaged drum instead of pulling it. One fisherman said he finds a drum lighter when it is full of lobster because there is less room for water. Drums are more expensive than traps, but they are said to fish better. Since they are expensive and fish well, they are stolen quite frequently.

Stealing

     All informants agreed that stealing from traps is
one of the most serious problems facing those who pull
traps for a living. According to one fisherman, the
problem is more serious every year, and an indication of
the escalation of stealing is that the thieves are
becoming more blatant. One young fisherman commented:
"Out of 325 fishermen in the co-op, I only know 50 who are
honest. Even my friends steal from traps. But I never
get mad when someone steals from my traps. I just check
the traps more often, and I try to vary the times I go out
so people don't know when I'll be there." Those who steal
are mainly younger men who have only a few traps (15 to
20) of their own or do not own any. When the quantity of
lobster begins to drop off in December, some other men who
may not be doing very well may also start hauling other
men's traps. One fisherman stated that he no longer hauls
traps and returned to line fishing because of the problem
of stealing. Another turned to running his hotel and
retired from fishing because the stealing made him so
angry.
     Those who steal know the location of each person's
territory and are familiar with a man's schedule for
hauling traps. They obtain this information through
inquiry and observation. They may ask about how well a
particular man is doing and when he checks the different
areas of his territory. For these reasons, most fishermen
are loathe to talk about their catches or their schedules.
To ensure a good catch, a thief will haul another man's
traps the day before the owner plans to haul. The
fishermen are aware of this strategy, and many avoid a
strict schedule in an effort to foil such attempts.
     Although they are hesitant to give names, islanders
generally know the identity of the thieves. For example,
it is suspicious when a man hauls traps and brings in
lobster but is never seen building traps. Or a man who
has only a few traps and yet leaves to haul them every day
will be suspected of hauling more than his own traps.
Occasionally a person is actually seen pulling someone
else's traps.
     There are several ways that a man can know if
someone has stolen from his traps. When a trap sits in
the water, the wood is covered with silt. If a diver
removes the lid of a trap and does not replace it in the
exact position as before, clean areas on the trap will be
exposed. Second, if a man hauls a trap that is black but

contains no lobster, he can be fairly sure that someone got to this trap before he did. Sometimes a fisherman will tack a loose lid to a trap and if he finds the nail missing, he suspects that he has been robbed.

Stealing from traps is a very sensitive topic, and people are reluctant to talk openly about it. Although many argue that stealing will one day lead to fights, ramming the thief's boat, and eventually a shooting, there seems to be a discrepancy between what people say will happen and what actually does happen. All are agreed that taking a thief to court is a waste of time.

Hernando, a successful fisherman with 150 traps, has come across the same person stealing from his traps on three different occasions. The first time, Hernando informed the thief that the traps were his, told him to leave, and said that he did not want to see him there again. The second time Hernando encountered the thief, he became angry and gave a serious warning. The third time he became incensed, threatening to knock the thief in the water, and to push his skiff away so that it would look like a drowning accident. Although islanders talk of cases where a thief's boat has been rammed, it is not clear that this has actually happened. No stealing-related shooting has ever taken place on Caye Caulker. In fact, some of the men take a fairly resigned attitude toward theft, and claim that stealing is simply part of lobster fishing and there is not much that can be done about it. One man reported:

> Sometimes people tell me when they see someone
> pulling my traps. But I tell them that since
> I did not see it happen, I'm not going to do
> anything about it. It doesn't bother me very
> much. I don't think it's worth killing anyone
> over this.

There are other ways that islanders use to discourage trap thieves. Often the Co-op will refuse to lend money to a 'known thief.' Islanders also refuse to participate in any kind of reciprocity with a thief. Thieves may be denied the normal courtesies and reciprocal favors. One day several men, one of whom is a 'known thief,' were sitting around together. The thief asked one of the men for a hit off a joint that was being passed around, and he was refused. The men began to ask the thief why he hauls traps every day when he only owns ten or fifteen traps. The thief laughed uneasily and asked for a cigarette but was told that he would get nothing. An open confrontation and expressions of disapproval such as this are very unusual on Caye Caulker.

Diving for Lobster

Since hauling traps is more profitable than diving, most of the fishermen who dive for their lobster are younger men or non-islanders who either cannot afford to buy traps or have been unable to acquire a territory. The men on Caye Caulker dive mostly inside the reef, although occasionally they will go out to the "blue", beyond the reef. The lobster are said to be larger and more plentiful outside the reef, but so are the sharks.

Equipment is simple and inexpensive. Divers use a mask, fins, and sometimes a snorkel, but they do not use Scuba gear. Snorkeling gear was introduced to the island about 15 years ago by foreigners. Sometimes the diver will also wear a shirt to keep warm while diving. Three different instruments are used to capture lobster. Some divers use the Hawaiian sling or a spear gun. While these are very accurate, they are expensive and will damage the meat unless the lobster is shot in the head. Also, spears can easily be lost and the points can be broken. The traditional, most commonly used instrument is a hook stick, which is about three feet long and has a large metal hook attached to the end with wire. The advantages of the hook stick are that it is cheap and easy to make. It is also more simple to use since it does not need to be reloaded. In addition, it puts only a very small hole in the lobster without visibly damaging the meat.

Lobster are found in the crevices of coral heads on the ocean bottom. To look for lobster the diver brings his face within inches of a crevice in the coral rock. The whole lobster is usually not visible because the lobster likes to remain hidden, but the antennae are easy to spot. In order to keep himself under the water or to maintain his position in a heavy current, the diver grabs onto the coral with his bare hands. He must watch for sea urchins, stinging corals, moray eels, and sharks.

Sleeping nurse sharks are often found under the very rocks that lobster prefer. Although they are not supposed to be a threat to man, most divers try to keep a respectful distance, especially if the sharks are larger than five feet. All divers who hook lobster or spear fish face sharks who in their search for food are attracted to the dying animal. One man remarked: "I share the water

with the sharks. We are both hunters. I won't dive if I
see sharks around, but if I dive and sharks appear I'll
just relax and try not to draw their attention. If
anything happens, well, that's life. I don't stop diving
because of sharks." Sharks can be seen on virtually every
diving trip.

There are three strategies for diving for lobster.
Sometimes a group of men go to an area far away and spend
a few weeks at a fishing camp. Men also dive regularly in
small groups in the general vicinity of the caye.
Finally, some men take tourists to the reef and collect
lobster and fish while the tourists are snorkeling.

1. <u>Camping</u>: Once in a while, men get together
and dive in camps. They leave the island for one to three
weeks and set up camp on a faraway caye. A camp is made
up of a small group of men who dive from early in the
morning until late in the afternoon. They take turns
cooking, each one being responsible for cooking for a day.
They take an absolute minimum of supplies avoiding even a
change of clothing, and live on fish for the most part.
Most men on Caye Caulker have at one time worked in camps.
They often recall these experiences with nostalgia. In
other parts of coastal Belize, such as San Pedro and
Placencia diving in camps is more common than on Caye
Caulker.

2. <u>Daily group dives</u>: Men will also go out in
small groups for the day and dive in the general vicinity
of the caye. Some of these groups meet regularly and
others are formed on a more ad hoc basis. They leave
between 6:30 and 7:30 in the morning and stay out until
early afternoon. Some groups will drop each man at a
certain distance from the boat where he will collect
lobster which he places on a float and drags along with
him as he works his way to the boat. At other times they
may anchor the boat in one spot and work that area before
moving on to another area. Jim Moreno dives regularly
with his younger brother. They employ a 'rock to rock'
method. They dive coral rocks that are isolated from
other rocks. Their premise is that rocks which stand
alone will contain a higher concentration of lobster since
it is the only available shelter in the area. They try to
choose rocks that are near a channel where lobster come in
from the blue. Often one man runs the boat while the
other dives. When they spot a rock they want to dive, one
man will jump in the water and scout the rock. If there
are only a couple of lobster, he will collect them by
himself and return to the boat. If there are many

lobster, the diver will signal to the other who then drops anchor and also dives the rock. The main disadvantage to this method is that a great deal more fuel is burned than if they were to drop anchor immediately and dive a large area before moving on.

      3. <u>Diving and Tourism</u>: Some men dive when they take tourists to the reef. These men are generally young, ranging from 15 to 30 years old. For the price of U.S. $3.00 per person, they will take a group of tourists to the reef for about three hours. They anchor the boat, and while the tourists swim around, they dive for lobster. After exhausting the area, they will move to a different spot. To work in this way, these men must have some way to attract tourists. Some have a sign posted on their house, such as 'Contact Sandy for Reef Trips Here.' Men also depend on having a trademark to attract tourists. Sandy has the reputation of partying with the tourists and is friendly with them. Robby's trademark is his sailboat which some tourists prefer to the motorized boats or skiffs. One man said that he always tries to be friendly with the tourists, and furthermore he intends to buy cushioned seats and a canopy for the boat since he knows tourists like that kind of luxury.

      When tourists first arrive on the island, they are often approached and offered a trip to the reef. Sometimes tourists choose to go out with the owner of their hotel or someone the owner has recommended, usually a relative. Occasionally there are more aggressive techniques. A man might ask tourists several times if they are interested in going to the reef, and some stand at the corner of a street and ask every tourist that goes by. A minimum number of tourists are required before a man will take a group out. Tourists who express an interest in going to the reef are often told that they are responsible for finding more tourists.

      A man who has a skiff and a motor can make a living taking tourists to the reef in combination with diving. But a man who does not own a skiff must borrow one, and this gives him a handicap. First of all, he must split the money he takes in with the owner of the boat. The owner generally takes a minimum of U.S.$7.50. Therefore, a man who does not own his boat must take larger groups of tourists in order to realize any profit. He is also dependent on the availability of a boat to borrow.

The Lobster Season

The lobster season begins July 15 and ends March 15. Catching lobster between March and July is illegal and punishable by fine. During the off season, the men who haul traps can build new traps and repair old ones. Wood for building traps is available on credit at the co-op. Just before the season opens, traps are put out in the water. Since no lobster can be sold until the first day of the season, traps cannot be put out too early. Some men store lobster in pens in the water, but this is risky because they can become very thin or 'mauger' if kept there too long. Others 'tail' the lobster and pack them in iceboxes, hidden deep in the mangrove swamps. These iceboxes are carefully guarded twenty-four hours a day.

At the beginning of the season, men check their traps frequently, often every other day, but by December the lobster catch begins to slack off. If catches diminish, fishermen start bringing in traps in December to clean and store them by their houses rather than leave them in the water where they will deteriorate.

When lobster are sold to the Co-op, the men receive a first payment, based on the weight of the lobster tails. On March 15 the men receive their 'second payment,' the co-op rebate, in a lump sum. This sudden influx of cash usually results in a drinking spree and a flurry of building activity. At this time families invest in building hotels, new houses at the cut for their grown children, and new skiffs. In June the co-op has its annual meeting featuring a big dance with a Reggae band and free food and drink for everyone on the island. At the annual meeting, new officers are elected, the annual report is presented to all shareholders, government officials give speeches on the current state of the fishing industry, and prizes are awarded to the most productive fishermen in four categories: lobster, scale fish, conch, and rock crab. Representatives from international companies wanting to purchase next year's lobster catch arrive with briefcases and business suits that present a stark contrast to the barefoot fishermen. Sealed bids are presented and opened. For the last few years, Red Lobster Inns of America has purchased the entire lobster catch for Caye Caulker. One year, however, a French restaurant chain was the successful bidder.

The Future of Lobster Fishing

In 1982 so many lobster were produced on Caye Caulker that the boat from Belize City had to come out each morning to take the daily catch to the processing plant. This (1982) was a record season with a 127% increase over the 1981 catch. The lobster catch rose from 121,175 pounds in 1981 to 275,275 pounds in 1982, while the price jumped from $15.04 to $18.13 Belize per pound, an increase of over 20 percent. The co-op's net profit was $368,068, an increase of 236 percent from the previous year.[3] It marked an incredible boom for Caye Caulker, and turned the islanders into some of the most affluent of Belizeans. At the Northern Fishermen Co-ops' annual meeting in June 1982, Mark Huesner was awarded a prize for bringing in the most lobster, 7,000 pounds, for an income of over U.S.$63,000. Anyone who took fishing seriously made more than U.S. $20,000 during the season.

The dramatic increase in production was due primarily to the 'Red Tide', which affected the coastal waters of Belize during August and September in 1980. This natural phenomenon is a result of a dense concentration of small plantlike organisms that create patches of toxic discolored water when they start to multiply in large numbers. While the toxin does not directly affect the lobster, it killed off many of the fish that feed on young lobster. Consequently, the lobster population exploded.[4]

In January 1983, islanders generally agreed that production was not up to the levels of the previous year. As nature slowly returned to equilibrium, the lobster population declined to previous levels. People hoped that any increase in fishing income would result from higher prices rather than increased production, but such was not the case. In 1983 the price of lobster dropped over 9 percent (see Table I). However, in 1984 and 1985 lobster production was up again, and the fishermen did well.

There are concerns on Caye Caulker that if fishermen were to continue increasing their production they would 'fish out' the waters around the caye. The establishment of a July 15 to March 15 lobster season is part of a government effort to prevent overfishing. Many islanders speculate about the apparent decrease in number of lobster at San Pedro on nearby Ambergris Caye. Lobster fishing has been severely reduced there, and the village of San Pedro generally has invested its future in tourism. But others do not agree that the lobster is really in danger.

Table I. The Lobster Catch, 1981-1983

Year	No. of Members of Co-op	Total Catch in Pounds	Price per lb.* (Belize dollar)	Total Net Profit of Co-op
1981	200	121,175	$ 15.04	$109,282.98
1982	235	275,275	$ 18.13	$368,068.74
1983	292	207,088	$ 16.49	$155,470.14
1984	337	274,132	$ 17.72	$224,768.40

Data from The Northern Fishermen Cooperative Annual Reports, 1982, 1983, 1984

* $ 1.00 Belize is equivalent to $.50 U.S.

One man commented: "There are two populations of lobster,
one which moves in a cyclical pattern and another that
lives in the Belize waters and doesn't move. The lobster
that lives here is being fished out, but the cyclical
population still remains strong."

There is a possibility that the increase in numbers
of lobster fishermen, attracted by the high profits
possible from lobster, may lead to overfishing.
Overfishing is reported to have occurred in the North
Atlantic, in the Bahamas, and around Florida and other
islands of the Caribbean.[5] The waters surrounding Caye
Caulker behind the barrier reef are fished intensely. As
these areas are now saturated with traps, enterprising
lobster fishermen are looking into the possibility of
lobster fishing outside the reef. Because this area has
never been fished intensely, no one knows how many lobster
are there. Laying and maintaining traps outside the reef
involves much greater risks to man and traps. Currents
are very strong and the water is deep; therefore, traps
are more likely to be lost, and heavier, more expensive
equipment is needed for this venture to be successful.
One young fisherman is experimenting with strong traps set
in water 50 feet deep outside the reef. The trap has a
buoy 3 feet from the surface so it can be spotted, is
larger than the traditional trap, and has two openings.
He maintains that these traps already are catching a
significantly greater number of lobster than inside the
reef.

On Caye Caulker, people believe that anything in the
sea belongs to any man who can obtain it. The idea of
conserving lobster stock is only just beginning to take
hold on Caye Caulker and other fishing islands. The
imposition of a lobster season, the prohibition on taking
berried lobsters (females with eggs), and a minimum size
(4 oz. tail) for legal sale all represent attempts to
protect the lobster breeding stock. Several common
practices on Caye Caulker indicate that these rules are
being ignored. Although undersized tails cannot be sold
to the co-op, they are regularly served up in local
restaurants. Fishermen sometimes scrape the eggs off a
berried lobster before taking it to the co-op to sell.
Finally, although the season begins officially on July 15,
some fishermen set their traps and store lobsters in pens
or in iceboxes, in order to bring in a large catch the
first day of the season.

Besides overfishing, there are other threats to the
future of lobster production. Traps lost during a storm

or pulled by a thief and not reset in such a way that the owner can find them continue to catch lobster. These lobster perish in the trap until it finally disintegrates, usually in a couple of years. In addition, lobster are highly sensitive to oil. Ships flush oil out of their tanks as they go up and down the coast of Belize, and this has an effect on the lobster population.

Obviously, existing regulations must be enforced for any lobster conservation program to be successful. On San Pedro enforcement of conservation laws is stepping up. In the spring of 1984, a restaurant was fined $500.00 for serving lobster out of season, and the police were reportedly watching boats at the reef with binoculars to spot any lobster being brought aboard. Enforcement of the legal size limit and of the season would go a long way towards improving the lobster breeding stock. One measure that Belize may have to consider in the future is to raise the legal size of the lobster to 4 1/4 ounces so that each lobster is ensured the chance to breed once before being caught. Most lobster are caught at the beginning of their maturity, which results in the loss of almost an entire generation each year. Raising the legal size would initially reduce the year's catch drastically but would ensure a greater future for lobster fishing.

Deep Sea Fishing

The Belizean government wants to encourage the development of a deep sea fishing industry, to exploit the rich and virgin territory outside the reef. The Belize Fishermen Cooperative Society, with the help of the United Nations CARE program, has undertaken several test programs for deep-sea fishing. In addition, they have attempted to develop new markets for scale fish. At the present, Jamaica is still the best scale fish market used by the Northern Fishermen Cooperative. At the opening address of the annual meeting of the co-op in 1983, Mr. Francis Gegg, a Belizean businessman, urged fishermen to consider diversifying into facets of the fishing industry beyond the shallow seabed. He stressed that current fishing areas are limited, seasonal, and overfished and do not allow for real growth and expansion. He pointed out that the bumper crop of the 1983 season was not the result of improved techniques but of an explosion in the lobster population, and suggested that the profits from 1983 be invested in deep-sea fishing equipment. However, because current fishing practices are relatively easy, bring in a good income, and involve little investment, the incentive to diversify is lacking.

Furthermore, deep-sea fishing does not appeal to most Caye Caulker fishermen for several reasons. First, it requires a cash investment in very expensive equipment, primarily a deep-sea fishing vessel with winch and pulley mechanisms for hauling lines and nets and sonar devices for finding schools of fish. Second, it requires a different approach to fishing. Fishermen on Caye Caulker like to fish close to home to return each day to the island, they traditionally work individually or in partnerships, and they keep a schedule that is relaxed and unpressured. If they are unable to check their traps one day, they can always do so the next. Deep-sea fishing with crews and equipment that must be in constant use would require a kind of commercial approach to fishing that has not yet developed on Caye Caulker.

Rather than develop the risky and more taxing deep sea fishing, most Caye Caulker fishermen are choosing to develop the burgeoning tourist industry. The tourist trade can provide an additional income that does not require great capital investment and can be adapted to family organization and the social values of the island far more readily than deep-sea fishing. An examination of the structure of families and the nature of family relationships, domestic groups, and support networks will demonstrate the ways that fishing and tourism are being combined to produce an economy that is compatible with island social organization.

NOTES

1.   See Craig, 1966, Chapters VI and VIII for a description of line fishing, use of fish nets, fish traps (also called <u>trampas</u> or heart weirs), and the fishing of loggerhead turtles, conch and crab.

2.   Acheson, James, <u>Anthropology of Fishing</u>, Annual Review of Anthropology, 1981, 10:285.

3.   <u>The Northern Fishermen Cooperative Annual Report</u>, 1982.

4.   "A Tapered Catch" <u>The New Belize</u>, July 1982, pages 4-6.

5.   Dippel, John "Looking for the Last Maine Lobster" <u>Oceans</u>, 13 Jan 1980, pp. 61-63, and personal communication, Edward Booth.

III

The Northern Fishermen
Cooperative Society

The islanders of Caye Caulker have access to some of the best fishing grounds in the Caribbean, particularly for lobster. They have exploited these resources in ways that are compatible with their particular social forms. At the same time they have developed strategies that have significantly improved their economic situation. A major strategy was the formation of the very successful Northern Fishermen Cooperative Society, Ltd. The aim of this chapter[1] is to describe these economic and social developments from the first settlement to the formation of the co-op.

In several ways, the historical development of Caye Caulker parallels the history of Belize, producing some of the same cultural patterns in both settings. First, like the rest of the Honduras Bay Settlement, the island was essentially uninhabited until one hundred years ago and therefore has had no long-established traditions. Further, when it was settled finally by Mestizo refugees from the Caste Wars of Yucatan in the 1870's, it developed in relative isolation from the mainland without significant 'official' colonial interest just as British Honduras developed in relative isolation from the British Caribbean. Distance from the colonial power on the mainland and the absence of ruling families with control of land contributed to the strong sense of independence and autonomy among the islanders to this day.

On Caye Caulker, unlike the mainland of Belize, the primary economic force has been fishing. The Mestizo

settlers brought with them from the Yucatan a cultural
system which was based on <u>milpa</u> farming. However, this
system was influenced both by the Creole culture of the
Caribbean area and by the change from farming to fishing.
Although the first settlers worked on coconut plantations
on Caye Caulker, fishing has played a larger role than
plantation work in shaping Caye Caulker's historical and
cultural development. Fishing fostered independence and
individualism: it involved little cooperative effort and
allowed each man to work independently. As a fisherman,
each man was his own boss. Moreover, slaves were never
brought in to work the coconut plantations, and thus Caye
Caulker avoided the master-slave hierarchy found elsewhere
in plantation systems. The present culture of Caye
Caulker is a synthesis of Yucatecan and Caribbean
traditions, tempered by a relatively egalitarian economic
system and focused on the family as the social institution
of primary loyalty.

Fishing, in combination with the islanders' emphasis
on autonomy and equality, has generated a particular
pattern of development on Caye Caulker. During the early
years of settlement, line fishing was supplemented by work
on coconut plantations as a means of income. The
development of commercial fishing drew the islanders more
and more into the fishing industry, lessening their
dependence on cocal work. At the same time, as the
industry grew and monopolies developed, the individualism
of Caye Caulker fishermen worked against them. For 30
years they lived at a subsistence level, selling their
produce to foreign monopolies who had exclusive control of
lobster and fish export quotas set by the Colonial
government. Recognizing the necessity of cooperating in
order to achieve collective economic independence from the
foreign monopolies, they formed the Northern Fishermen
Cooperative Society, Ltd. and struggled to win their own
export license from the colonial government.

The successful development of the cooperative has
been the means by which Caye Caulker fishermen obtained
their collective economic independence. In 1960, when the
government officially registered the cooperative and
granted it an export quota, the members began exporting
large amounts of lobster immediately. They were no longer
producing for an exporter; rather, they were working for
themselves. Within a few years they had expanded co-op
operations to include producing, processing, and
negotiating contracts, as well as exporting lobster and
fish. Over the last two decades they have secured

successively higher prices for lobster and have increased production so that today incomes average between U.S.$10,000 and $12,000 with top producers making over U.S.$40,000 in a year.

The economic and social development of Caye Caulker has been a process of change from subsistence fishing to commercial fishing, primarily through the development of the lobster industry. Islanders proudly claim that Caye Caulker is the wealthiest village in Central America. The extent to which this is true is a result of the success of the fishing co-op.

Early History

Tracing the early history of Caye Caulker has been difficult. First of all, nothing has yet been written on the topic, so there are no secondary sources on which to rely. Furthermore, there are few surviving records. In answer to inquiries about land deeds and old maps at the Lands Office in Belize City, the gentleman behind the desk replied that they had none and suggested that only the islanders themselves knew about the island's history. Others who have attempted to trace Caye Caulker's history seem to have encountered the same problem. Craig, in his Geography of Fishing in British Honduras and Adjacent Coastal Areas, notes that "specific dates are lacking."[2] Consequently, this history is based on the islanders' accounts of the settlement of Caye Caulker, supplemented with the little printed information that is available.

There is no evidence of a Mayan settlement on Caye Caulker during the rise or peak of the Mayan empire in Belize, probably because of the mangrove swamps that covered much of the island. However, there were fishing settlements on Ambergris Caye and Caye Chapel,[3] and it is likely that the Mayans living on the neighboring islands visited Caye Caulker, as the islanders report having found old tools and pottery on the caye.

In the ninth and tenth centuries A.D., the Mayans suddenly migrated north to Yucatan, and all of these fishing settlements were abandoned. Spanish explorers who sailed along the coastline in the early 1500's found it virtually uninhabited. Since the Spanish were not interested in settling the Belizean coast, it remained uninhabited until the seventeenth century, when buccaneers established a settlement on St. George's Caye near Belize City.[4]

Although Caye Caulker was still uninhabited, it was visited during these centuries by fishermen from Mexico, who put ashore for fresh water from a "big hole" on the caye. Islanders cite some evidence that 'pirates' were on or around Caye Caulker as well: an anchor from that time period was found in the channel at the south end of the island and an old wreck was discovered off the south end of Caye Chapel.

1870-1932: Establishment of a Settlement

With the exception of St. George's Caye near Belize City, the offshore islands were still uninhabited as late as the 1830's.[5] Then with the outbreak of the Caste Wars of Yucatan in 1848, thousands of Spanish and Mestizos fled across the border into Belize seeking refuge. Some filtered down through Ambergris Caye and San Pedro to Caye Caulker. It is likely that many of these first immigrants had fished in these areas and perhaps camped on these islands earlier.[6] Today, many of the islanders trace their family histories as far back as the Caste Wars and remember the region in Mexico from which their ancestors originated.

Though dates for the settlement of Caye Caulker are uncertain, Eduardo Reyes, the great-grandson of the man who purchased the island, pieced together part of the story of its settlement. Eduardo's great-grandfather Luciano Reyes sailed from Spain to the coast of the Yucatan peninsula, where he became a logwood cutter. He was forced to flee Mexico during the Caste Wars and migrated south to Belize. He settled in San Pedro on Ambergris Caye and entered the intense land speculation over the island, hoping to purchase the entire caye. He lost. On 13 September 1869, James Hume Blake became the successful bidder and purchased nearly all of Ambergris for a sum of $625 Bz.[7] Having lost out in the speculation over Ambergris, Luciano Reyes decided to buy the island of Caye Caulker. He paid the government $300 Bz. for it.

After taking possession of the island, Reyes sold the northern third to a man named Henderson from the Caribbean. A few families, refugees from Yucatan, who had been living on San Pedro, moved to the island and also bought land from Reyes. Their small plots were scattered among the larger lots which were purchased by wealthy Belizeans, who visited the island only for vacations and hired the small landowners to care for their property and buildings during the rest of the year. Eventually the original landowners of large areas of the island died, and their heirs sold land to the families who now live on Caye Caulker.

Families often were very large, and family-owned land was divided up as the children grew up, married, and formed households of their own. Bonds between family members were very strong, both emotionally and economically. Children built houses close to those of their parents either through land inherited from their parents or by purchasing land nearby. For example, the land which remained in Luciano Reyes' hands was passed down in the family until today it is divided among his grandson, and two of his great-grandsons, who live on adjoining lots.

At this time the 'streets' were laid out on Caye Caulker (map 4). The village layout is typical of the Mestizo area of northern Belize. It is long and narrow, with two main streets, referred to as the Front and Back streets, running parallel to the coast. Along these two streets the houses are arranged. The first houses built by the settlers were small clapboard or thatched houses with thatched roofs. Each family had one small building for sleeping and a second which served as a kitchen. They originally cooked over coconut husk fires, but later began to use butane stoves when they could afford them. They preserved their fish by salting, drying, or smoking it, much as the buccaneers had done earlier.

"The industry, as the island was settled, was cocal," according to Eduardo Reyes. On Caye Caulker, the cocals were owned by Reyes and Henderson. Cocals were planted on Ambergris Caye in the 1880's and 1890's by the owner Blake and his business partners, and it is probable that the coconut plantations on Caye Caulker would have been planted at approximately the same time. Establishing a cocal required a large capital outlay for expenses such as clearing the land, digging the holes, gathering seaweed for fertilizer, and planting seedlings. Once a cocal was planted, workers were required to keep them cleared of underbrush, to pick the coconuts, and to husk and deliver the nuts to Belize City. Most of the settlers could not afford to go into the business, so they became laborers on the cocals, working for wages in order to supplement their subsistence fishing. According to Eduardo's description, "From north to south, wherever coconut trees could grow, they were grown. The workers would start at the north end, husking the coconuts and filling the boats, and work their way to the south end. By the time they finished, they would have to start all over . . . The trees produced continually." The coconuts were sold primarily to Blake and his partners in Belize City, who owned and completely dominated the cocal industry on Ambergris Caye.

Caye Caulker's cocals were never worked by slaves, as slavery had been abolished before they were planted. Furthermore, the owner of the cocal, Reyes, was of the same racial and ethnic background as the laborers. This ethnic homogeneity and the absence of a slavery system precluded the development of the typical Caribbean plantation hierarchy based on race and class. On the other hand, status and wealth differences developed between land owners and wage laborers.

The islanders, primarily wage laborers, used cash income from cocal work to buy fruit, vegetables, and other necessities to supplement their subsistence fishing. However, the income from cocal work was very small. One woman remembered her family working on the cocal when she was a small. "They would work for hours with those dumb coconuts and get only pennies. It was a very hard life and we were very poor."

The long hours of hard work for little return necessitated some type of support system to help the islanders make ends meet. Reciprocal exchange networks developed to ensure their survival in hard times. These ties were strongest among family members, but applied to interfamily relations as well. If someone brought in a big catch of fish, others would help him with it, knowing that they would be given a few fish to take home. Later, they would reciprocate with fish or some kind of produce or labor. People who owned any kind of fruit tree distributed the fruit when it ripened, knowing they would be repaid later. In this way goods and services were distributed evenly among the island families, and although they were all poor, group cooperation acted as a kind of insurance against times of want.

Fishing, balanced with dependence on kin support networks, was a means for each man to provide for his own family, but it was primarily a subsistence endeavor. Fish occasionally were sold in Belize City, but brought in very little cash. Nonetheless, fishing was preferred to cocal work. It was less strenuous and time consuming and allowed greater independence. When it came to fishing, each man was his own boss. Hand-lining was the primary fishing technique on Caye Caulker, and it required only one man and a fishing line. Without more complex technology, there was no need for teams or crews. As the

Belizean fishing smacks were rather small, two or three people were the maximum number that could fish together on the same boat. With the later advent of lobster traps, two became the most efficient number for cooperative fishing arrangements. Furthermore, men who did fish together divided the catch among themselves rather than working for wages. They were not working for anyone else; they were working with them. Moreover, if they did fish with someone else, it was usually a relative. Fishing as the primary mode of production reinforced the characteristics of individualism and autonomy which were generated by Caye Caulker's isolation.

Early on, the islanders asserted this independence and self-sufficiency in response to a system whose nonegalitarian nature was not to their liking. They were affiliated with the mainland through the Alcalde system of government, a traditional Mayan form of local government whereby a village is headed by an elected leader called the Alcalde who reports to the central government. The system was tailored to the needs of Mayan farming villages which required a leader to coordinate a schedule of work. It appears that the system was neither as elaborate nor as strong on Caye Caulker, where relatively few group decisions were necessary and where loyalty to one's family took precedence over community spirit, even during the most difficult times. The man elected Alcalde of Caye Caulker served primarily as a liaison with Belize City. He was accorded so little authority by the other islanders that when he ordered a work party, people simply did not show up. He was required to report to the Colonial Government in Belize City, and by the 1920's or 1930's, it had become apparent to the Colonial officials that he was having difficulty fulfilling his role. They decided to abandon the Alcalde system and sent out a policeman to act as the official representative of the government on Caye Caulker. This system did not prove to be much more effective.

Beginning and Growth of the Lobster Industry

The shift in emphasis from subsistence to commercial fishing, which has played the largest role in shaping the caye's development, is connected with the initiation and expansion of the lobster industry in the 1920's. At the beginning of the twentieth century, spiny lobster were abundant in the seabed around Caye Caulker, where the shallow, warm coastal waters provided an ideal habitat.

Islanders tell stories of lobster crawling up on the beaches in such numbers that they were considered "rubbish" food. So, in spite of its abundance, Belizean fishermen had little use for the spiny lobster prior to the 1920's. They had no equipment for catching lobster and had to gather them by hand.

Then in 1921, Captain R. E. Foote arrived in Belize. He was a representative of the Canadian Franklin Baker Company, a major exporter of coconuts.[8] When he discovered the large, untouched lobster population, he began experimenting with the type of lobster pot that was used in the maritime provinces of Canada. His experiment was successful enough to warrant setting up a business. Captain Foote recruited a group of Creole fishermen from Belize City, taught them to build, set, and haul lobster traps[9] and set up a canning plant on a barge near Water Caye.

By 1925 a scarcity of lobster around Water Caye led Captain Foote to relocate his barge further north near the windward entrance to Baldwin's Bogue. After relocating, the canners' volume of production increased, but disputes arose between Foote and the fishermen who supplied him with lobster. The fishermen were paid only 1 cent per pound for their lobster, and they began agitating for a better price.[10] The quantities of lobster they brought to the cannery became "erratic." In 1931, the conflict over lobster prices came to an abrupt halt, when the barge and cannery were destroyed in a hurricane.

By 1932 Captain Foote had acquired a second barge with a packing plant, which he established in the leeward bay at Caye Caulker. Starting from scratch again, he trained local fishermen to build, set, and haul the Canadian-style lobster traps. Initially production was high, as the seabeds around Caye Caulker were virgin territory. It has been established that at the peak of the plant's operations, twelve fishing smacks and approximately 25 processors were employed in the production of lobster.[11] However, after a strong start, the industry began to falter because of fluctuating market conditions in the United States. The depression in the United States deepened and prices fell. By 1935 Captain Foote had abandoned his Caye Caulker operation.

Although the export market had largely disappeared, Caye Caulker fishermen continued to catch lobster for home consumption or for sale in the Belize City marketplace. During this slow period they experimented with the design of the Canadian lobster traps and produced a modified version which was more suitable to the Caribbean environment. During the 1930's, a few freezer boats began cruising the Belizean coast, buying whole lobster from the Caye Caulker fisherman for 1 to 1 1/2 cents per pound and exporting them to the States.[12] However, the fishermen did not produce much lobster because the prices were so low. Along with the cocal work, they continued to depend on line fishing, selling their catch in Belize City.

As the U.S. began to recover from the depression in the 1940's, exporting lobster by freezerboats became more profitable. By 1948 a couple of freezer boats and a seaplane, the Catalina, were exporting lobsters from the Belizean cayes and paying fisherman 5 to 7 cents per pound for them.[13] Lobster production increased slowly, as the prices were still quite low, and the islanders had become very wary of foreign operators. Their experience with the seaplane Catalina was a powerful lesson to both Caye Caulker and San Pedro fishermen.

> The buyers paid between 5 and 7 cents per pound for the lobsters, but they were bought on credit. No money was paid to the fishermen until the buyers returned to the island after delivering their cargo to purchasers in the United States. These purchasers were seasonal, and at the end of one season the "Catalina" flew off to the States with four thousand pounds of lobsters. It was never again seen by the villagers, who, to this date, have not been paid for this last load. It is an experience they have also, to this date, never forgotten.[14]

In spite of the exploitative practices of the exporters, lobster production continued to grow. The market for lobster in the U.S. had been firmly established, and lobster fishing became increasingly profitable. With both demand and prices rising, the islanders began to rely more on lobster fishing and less on low-paying cocal work. Both the profits and the independence afforded by fishing made it far more attractive than cocal work. Consequently, the cocal industry began to decline. Many trees damaged in storms and hurricanes were simply not replaced, and the coconut industry gradually disappeared on Caye Caulker. Even as late as the 1960's however, some coconuts were still produced for sale.

The 1940's also marked the beginning of a strong credit union and cooperative movement in Belize, led by a Jesuit priest, Father Marion Ganey. Father Ganey visited Caye Caulker in the late 1940's to discuss with the islanders the creation of a fishing cooperative, but little interest was generated in the idea. At that time, the market for fish and lobster was not well developed, so prices were low. Also, the fishermen worked alone or with just one partner, usually a family member, and cooperative production seemed neither necessary nor practical to them. However, thirty islanders did decide to form a credit union and managed to amass a total share capital of $3,608.60 Bz[15]. The credit union did not survive very long, however. Islanders give two reasons for its collapse. First, they were not very cash-oriented at the time. They had few dealings with the cash economy of the nonisland world, relying for the most part on their own food-gathering skills and on reciprocal exchanges with family and close friends. Second, the islanders had little knowledge of or experience with managing and using such an organization.

Development of the Foreign Monopoly

By 1949, the British colonial government in Belize recognized the increasing importance of lobster exports and began to impose export duties and issue export licenses for lobster. Early in 1950, B.H. Seafoods Ltd., owned by John Bilnik of the United States and Guy Nord of Belize, began buying lobster tails from Caye Caulker fishermen for 7 cents a pound, the highest price paid up to this time.[16] Shortly thereafter, two Belizeans, George Alamilla and Alfonso Gutierrez, and an American, Ernest Baker, formed Caribbean Queen Seafood Ltd. They began a price war with B.H. Seafoods, driving the price for lobster to as much as 16 cents a pound.[17] Within a few months, the two companies decided to merge in order to end the price war that was devastating to both. They applied to the colonial government for an exclusive export quota in order to create a monopoly. They were refused, partly because Caye Caulker fishermen voiced their opposition to such a concession.[18] The two companies completed the merger in spite of this and then were acquired by Colony Club Fisheries Ltd., headed by a Belizean, Harrison Courtenay.

Late in 1950 another company, Del Caribe Fisheries, owned by Ed Devorak, an American, emerged to compete with

Colony Club. Again, competition was short-lived and Colony Club sold out to Del Caribe. With this sale, Ed Devorak gained control of the only two companies with export licenses, created an effective monopoly, and could set his own prices. The fishermen had nowhere else to sell their lobster.[19]

Formation of the Co-op

For eight years Caye Caulker fishermen continued to supply Devorak's companies with lobster in exchange for very little compensation; however, they were becoming increasingly dissatisfied with the arrangement. They were aware that lobster prices on the international market were much higher than the price they received from Devorak. In the late 1950's Louis Sylvestre, local representative to the Legislative Assembly and PUP member, visited Caye Caulker to encourage the islanders to form a fishing cooperative. The idea suggested by Father Ganey a decade earlier appeared more promising, and by 1958 they were ready to take action to better their economic position. Henry Usher, then Registrar of Cooperatives, was invited to visit Caye Caulker to advise them on the mechanics of organizing a producers' cooperative. The process of overcoming traditional barriers to cooperation, like the islanders' extreme individualism, involved many visits by Dr. Usher and much discussion among islanders. Finally a small group of islanders drafted a proposal to form a co-op with a share capital of $662 Bz.[20] Next, they applied to the government for an export quota. According to one source, the government refused their application on two grounds: they were not yet officially registered as a cooperative, and the government believed that the fishermen were not yet able to manage their own business.[21]

Though they had lost the first round, this group of islanders was now convinced of the necessity of forming a co-op and was unwilling to give up. Tension between the producers and the exporter continued, escalating to open confrontation at the beginning of the 1960 season. The story of this confrontation is somewhat confusing. The Customs Department determined that the 1960-61 lobster season would open July 15, with purchasing beginning the sixteenth. However, on July 14, Colony Club and Del Caribe announced on the radio that although they would purchase lobster from most Belizean fishermen on the sixteenth, they would not buy from Caye Caulker or San

Pedro fishermen until the next day, July 17. The reasons behind this action are not clear. It is possible that Devorak, aware of the Caye Caulker fishermen's plans to create a marketing co-op, wanted to discourage them. At any rate, the announcement was made at night, so the islanders did not hear it.

Before they heard the message on the fifteenth, Caye Caulker fishermen had already hauled in huge amounts of lobster. It is customary for them to set their traps in the water one to two weeks early, so the first day's harvest is always the largest of the season. Once hauled in, the lobster will spoil, and since they had no storage facilities on the island, they were faced with disaster if they waited until the seventeenth to deliver their catch. The fishermen, organized now and working together, refused to take a loss. Determined to take control of the situation, they decided to send their lobster to Belize City through their unregistered co-op and confront Devorak.

The first shipment of lobster arrived at Del Caribe pier on the sixteenth. Devorak was initially unwilling to accept the shipment, but after lengthy bargaining he purchased the shipment at 16 cents a pound. Del Caribe purchased four more shipments of Caye Caulker lobster under the same terms. However, by the time the sixth shipment arrived, Devorak realized that he was seriously undermining his position by continuing to purchase lobster from the unregistered co-op. According to Godfrey,

> The ball was in his court. He either had to
> back down and hand the cooperative a victory
> or force the confrontation a step further. He
> must also have realized that he could not
> afford to hand the cooperative a victory so
> early. If he did not nip the cooperative
> movement in the bud now, it would end by
> eventually destroying him.[22]

Devorak announced that he would pay 1 cent less per pound, diverting the 1 cent to his agent on Caye Caulker rather than dealing directly with the unregistered cooperative. The fishermen refused his offer. They took the sixth shipment to Colony Club Fisheries, in hopes of a better price; however, Colony Club offered them even less. The fishermen refused this offer as well and decided to boycott both companies. Though determined not to sell to either of Devorak's companies, without an export license, they were unable to export the lobster themselves. They had to find somewhere to store it.

At this point the fishermen went to another American, Bucher Scott, who managed Baymen Fisheries Ltd. He agreed to store the lobster in his freezer until the fishermen could obtain an export quota. He also loaned them money on the security of the lobster he held in cold storage. He continued this policy for each shipment the fishermen delivered, enabling them to maintain their families and continue producing while carrying on their boycott of Devorak's companies.

The fishermen persisted in their attempt to obtain an export license, while, rumor has it, the American companies exerted pressure on the colonial government to deny the Caye Caulker co-op an export license. The struggle continued until a Canadian expert on cooperatives visited the colony. During his visit, Henry Usher invited the proposed co-op to send two members to a seminar at which they were allowed to present their case. When he learned of their situation, this expert asserted that the Caye Caulker fishermen should have been allowed to register as a cooperative society long ago.[23]

Shortly thereafter, on 5 September 1960, they were registered as the Northern Fishermen Cooperative Society Ltd. Citing the advice of the Canadian expert, the government granted the new co-op an export license. Through cooperation and perseverance the Caye Caulker fishermen had overcome the American monopoly and won economic independence. They were able to export the 40,000 pounds of lobster they held in storage and pay off the loans Bucher Scott had made them.[24]

Hurricane Hattie hit in 1961, just as the cooperative was getting off the ground. Though Hattie was one of the most vicious storms to hit Belize in years, it was just one of 21 which have ravaged the coast of Belize since 1787.[25] The devastation in Belize City was among the worst in its history, but even on Caye Caulker most of the houses that had been built along the windward shore were flattened by the storm surge in Hattie's wake. The thatched-roof houses were unable to withstand the force of the storm, and there were no cement buildings in which to seek shelter and safety. Hattie swept in from the blue with such force that she cut a channel straight through Caye Caulker. More than a dozen lives were lost, many of them children who were killed when the schoolhouse was picked up by the wind. The islanders remember Hattie

well, but they repeat their tales without relish, for
their losses were great.

> I was six years old at the time. Remember it
> like it was yesterday. It was terrible. All
> the houses, or nearly all the houses were
> blown away. We were in Tom Young's house
> with the roof tied down. I was sittin' under
> this table, a-praying like mad, praying more
> than I ever did, that I wouldn't be killed.
> Then we had to untie the roof and away it
> went, just like that. You see, if we hadn't
> untied it, we all would have blown away. Then
> we were in the center of the storm; there's
> about an hour when you're in the eye of the
> storm when its all still and we moved to
> another house. Good thing, too, that house of
> Tom's, it was blown clean away.

It took Caye Caulker a few years to recover fully
from Hattie.   During the 1961-62 season, although the
young co-op had suffered substantial losses because of
Hurricane Hattie, they continued to sell lobster to Baymen
Fisheries.   The coop received a government loan which
enabled it to import materials for new traps and
equipment, and by the end of the year it was back on its
feet with 53 members and a share capital of $2,221.94.
However, Baymen Fisheries offered a lower price for the
following season, and the co-op began looking for
somewhere else to sell its lobster.   Eager to become
completely independent, they approached the Metropolitan
Shrimp Exchange with a proposal to build their own
freezing plant in Belize City.   The Exchange agreed to
sponsor the project, and the plant was completed and in
operation by August of 1962.[26]
The co-op had achieved complete independence: it was
able to manage the whole process of producing, processing,
packing, and marketing lobster itself.   Moreover, it did
this well enough to meet the standards of the U.S. Food
and Drug Administration.   Furthermore, during the 1962-63
season, the co-op was able to pay member fishermen 10
cents more per pound plus a rebate.   By 1964 they were
selling their lobster tails in the United States for $2.10
Bz. a pound, an increase over the price Devorak had paid
them of more than 1000%.[27]   They had proven that they
could manage the whole operation autonomously, eliminating
middlemen and securing better prices for themselves.

From Subsistence to Affluence

The first ten year period of the co-op, between 1962 and 1972, was a time of strengthening the position of the co-op. Founding members such as Filemon and Beto Pariente, Tony Vega, Emelito, Ernesto and John Marin, Marciano and Teodoro Allen, Orlando Carrasco, Thomas Young, Cecilio, Jesus, and Rodolfo Heredia, Rojelio Novelo, Crispin Rosado, and Fernanco and Ismael Magana concentrated on increasing production and learning how to run the fledgling organization. Several men were sent abroad to learn fishing techniques and management practices. Income from lobster improved as the fishermen honed their skills in negotiating successful contracts abroad.

After this initial period of gradual improvement, the production of lobster began to be a truely profitable business. This was due to several factors. As the size of the co-op increased, the larger numbers of producers meant that the Caye Caulker contract was a more valuable commodity abroad, and the co-op itself could realize greater profits both for the producers and for the needs of the organization. These needs were an ability to give loans to members to improve their production and to build a marina and processing plant in Belize City. A larger size meant a more viable organization. A second equally important factor was the increase in demand for lobster on the world market and the consequent steady rise in the international price of lobster. Consequently from approximately 1975 onwards, the Caye Caulker fishermen began to realize large incomes. Furthermore, the Managing Committee of the co-op began to have an important role in the distribution of wealth on the island.

Current Organization and Function of the Co-op

The co-op operates as a producer-owned processor and distributor. Lobster, fish, conch, and crab which the members catch are brought to the receiving station on Caye Caulker or in Belize City. There the catch is weighed, and the fisherman receives an invoice for the initial payment per pound. The co-op puts out checks for initial payments once a week in Belize City. Produce received at Caye Caulker is sent to Belize City, where most of it is processed for export and shipped abroad. At the end of the fiscal year the dividends are distributed among

58

producing members, and they receive a final payment or
rebate per pound for their produce.

Membership

From the original membership of about 15 men, the
Northern Fishermen Co-op has grown to 337 members at the
close of the 1984 season. Two hundred ninety-seven of
those were producing members. During 1983 they accepted
59 new members and in 1984 there were 51 new members.
Membership has approximately tripled in the last five
years. Though many new members come from Caye Caulker
families, many others have been drawn to the co-op because
of rising lobster prices and the co-op's consistently high
profits. During the 1984 season, the co-op in Sarteneja,
in northern Belize on the Bay of Chetumal, folded and
became a member of the Northern Fishermen Cooperative.
Also twenty-five fishermen from San Pedro have dropped out
of San Pedro's Caribena Co-op to join the more profitable
Northern Fishermen co-op.

The Sarteneja Co-op folded partly because it was not
well-managed and partly for purely practical reasons of
location. Fishing grounds around Sarteneja are poor, so
the co-op members were forced to travel to southern Belize
to fish. They do mostly line fishing for scale fish, and
they must carry ice on their boats to keep the fish fresh.
However, when they operated out of the co-op at Sarteneja,
by the time they had made the trip to the fishing grounds
the ice was half-melted, so they were not able to fish
very long. They began bringing their fish into Belize
City to the Northern Fishermen Co-op plant rather than
making the trip all the way back to Sarteneja. This
allowed them to fish a little longer and produce a little
more. They soon realized that it would be more efficient
and profitable for them to join the Northern Fishermen Co-
op, which would allow them to purchase ice at Caye Caulker
or Belize City en route to the fishing grounds and deliver
their catch to the plant in Belize City on the way home.
Finally the Northern Fishermen Co-op is managed better and
gives a higher price. For these reasons, in 1983 the
Sarteneja Co-op folded and joined the Northern Fishermen
Co-op as a single member, with a single vote.

San Pedro fishermen who joined the Northern
Fishermen Co-op, were prompted to do so by the greater
profits it realized. The motive of increased income must
have been very strong, as the rivalry between the
communities of Caye Caulker and San Pedro is intense.

Although some San Pedranos have set aside this rivalry in the interests of larger profits, their relations with fellow San Pedranos have suffered as a result. Caye Caulker natives report that San Pedranos who have joined the Northern Fishermen Co-op have trouble even borrowing a wrench from neighbors.

It is not difficult to become a member of the Northern Fishermen Cooperative. Whereas most co-ops organized in Belize were local, this co-op was the first and was originally intended to serve the whole of Belize. Thus, any Belizean can apply to the co-op Managing Committee for membership. Currently, most members come from either Caye Caulker or Belize City. The applicant must have, or have access to, a licensed boat. Also, according to one Belizean who joined the co-op, "Your reputation is important, and how well known you are. By the time I applied for membership, I'd been fishing awhile. I was known to be a hard worker, especially by the people on the board, so I had no trouble getting in." At the age of sixteen, one can become a junior member, who gets neither voting rights nor a second payment on his produce. He is on trial for one year and must catch at least 300 pounds of lobster, conch, or fish. According to one fisherman, this is not very difficult: "If you can't produce that amount of fish, man, you are in the wrong business. You won't make enough to feed your family."

The co-op realizes the Caye Caulker ideals of independence through local control. Though members of the Managing Committee are most actively involved in running the co-op, all members may attend the general meetings to vote or voice concerns. The Managing Committee is usually composed of men from the same main island families each year, ensuring local Caye Caulker control of the co-op. Occasionally, someone suggests hiring an agent to negotiate contracts for the co-op on the international market in hopes of getting a little better price, but the motion is always voted down. Likewise, they proudly tell a story about a recent conference on the fishing industry in the Caribbean to which the Northern Fishermen Co-op sent a couple of members as representatives. Most of the other companies or co-operatives were represented by the lawyers who handle their affairs. The Caye Caulker representatives were the only fishermen at the conference, and they describe with delight the lawyers' amazement that a group of fishermen could collectively run a successful business, from production to marketing and exporting.

Older members express some concern that younger members may not be involved enough in the co-op. The Managing Committee is dominated by older members, who remember the struggles with foreign companies before the co-op was formed. The younger generation lacks this experience and has grown up with an easier life. They still value independence, but the question for the future will be whether they understand the implications of the co-op and their responsibilities to it. A key to securing their involvement in the co-op is keeping them informed and impressing upon them the importance of their role in the decision-making process. Currently, younger fishermen do not seem to feel they have sufficient clout to suggest changes.

Though the co-op is managed primarily by a committee which is elected from the membership, two regular general meetings are held each year and special meetings may be called. These provide forums for members to discuss issues and solutions and keep informed about the co-op's operations. The annual meeting, held after the close of the season in June or early July, is particularly important in implementing the co-op's desire to keep its members involved with and informed about its activities. During the morning meeting, which is closed to nonmembers, members review the co-op's operations during the previous fiscal year, its current financial situation, and the proposed budgets for the upcoming season. Though most decisions are made during the year by the Managing Committee, at this meeting, members have the opportunity to ask questions and bring up concerns. During the afternoon session, which is open to anyone, there are guest speakers, raffles, and awards for the top producers of lobster, conch, fish, and crab claws. Nominations for and elections to the Managing Committee are also held. The turnout for the annual meeting on Caye Caulker is very large. On Caye Caulker, where people are unaccustomed or unwilling to attend meetings for other organizations, such as the Village Council, the attendance at the co-op meeting is unusually large and indicates the top priority of the co-op among island organizations and the stake the islanders feel they have in managing its affairs.

Facilities and Employees

The Northern Fishermen Cooperative maintains facilities both on Caye Caulker and in Belize City. The co-op receiving station on Caye Caulker is at the back of the island, next to the back pier. It is a two-story cement building with facilities for weighing the fish and lobster and storing them on ice. The day-to-day operations at the receiving station are managed by Juni Zaldivar and his assistant, Choppy. Juni is a former boat builder and fisherman. As the cost of materials for boat building escalated, his profession became less profitable. Concerned about raising his family on a dwindling income, he accepted the job as manager of the Caye Caulker receiving plant five years ago.

Juni arrives at the co-op Monday through Saturday around 6:30 a.m. to start the ice machine and sell gas and oil to fishermen on their way out to fish. The island fishermen buy their gas and any parts they need for their boats or motors from the co-op, and the charges are billed to their accounts, so Juni must keep records of what he sells. At about 8:30, he radios the processing plant in Belize City to relay the amounts of gas and oil sold and the amount of produce received on the previous day. Then he closes up and goes home, returning again after lunch. Throughout the afternoon, fishermen bring in their catches. Juni must check their quality, weigh them, and write up product invoices for each. He may sell some ice, fish, or more gas. Around 6:00 p.m., when the last fisherman has brought in his product, Juni packs the fish and lobster on ice in the cold room, turns off the ice machine, and goes home. About once a week, or more often at the height of the season, he goes in at 6 a.m. to load the week's catch on the boat which transports it to the processing plant in Belize City.

The marina in Belize City is larger and still growing. There is a processing plant, which is managed by the Executive Secretary, another co-op employee. There, most of the product is frozen, sorted, packed, and shipped out. The Belize City marina also has a new wharf, which was financed completely by the co-op's own resources. The co-op is also in the process of constructing a new building expressly for ice production, to provide the greater quantities which will be necessary to accommodate the growing membership and expansion into deep-sea fishing. This is a more costly venture and has been financed by external loans.

Most of the product is exported; however, the Belizean government requires the co-op to sell some of its product locally to prevent the type of problem that has occurred in other parts of the Caribbean with the rise of commercial fishing. As a result of the much greater profits which can be realized by exporting fish, the fish disappear from the local market and the quality of the local diet drops. The co-op must sell its lobster on the local market at a loss, as the price they may charge is set by the government at U.S. $1.85 a pound, while the international price in 1984 is U.S. $8.86 a pound.

Managing Committee

The Managing Committee oversees the co-op's annual operations and has considerable power in making important decisions affecting the future of the co-op. This board consists of seven producing members, who are elected by their peers. Every year at the annual meeting, four new committee members are elected. The three who receive the most votes serve two-year terms, and the other serves a one-year term. There is no limit to the number of terms one can serve in office: "You can serve for as long as the people want you." Beto Pariente, for example, served for 23 years and Santiago Marin has been on the Managing Committee for twelve years. The Committee tends to be composed mainly of middle-aged to older fishermen, who have consistently produced large quantities of fish and have developed reputations for honesty and hard work. Most of them come from Caye Caulker. Their primary responsibilities are to decide on new members, decide on loan applications to existing members, and to handle marketing. They meet regularly on the first Monday of each month, but average about twenty meetings per year.

The committee oversees daily operations through the Executive Secretary in Belize City and the manager of the receiving station on Caye Caulker. One member is delegated responsibility for the Caye Caulker plant, and Juni Zaldivar reports any problems to him. The Executive Secretary reports any problems with the Belize City plant and works as a liaison between members and the Committee. Members come to him with complaints about plant operation, and he presents their concerns to the committee. The Committee then decides how to handle the complaint.

Loan requests are also channelled through the Executive Secretary, although the Committee itself approves or rejects them. Members can apply for loans to repair or purchase fishing equipment up to the amount at which their product for the current season is valued. There have been problems in the past with some fishermen not paying off their loans and others using them for personal projects, so the co-op is attempting to get tougher on its loan policies. Delinquent loan payments are a problem from time to time. The fishermen do not like to meddle in one another's financial affairs. Thus the co-op is generally lax about imposing any type of sanction for this offense, other than sending out notes to those with delinquent loans, requesting their payment.

The Committee also oversees the budgeting and administers the Education Fund, which was established to assist members' children in obtaining a high school education, to send members to Nova Scotia to participate in a deep-sea fishing training program, and to enable directors and members to attend seminars.

Apart from overseeing co-op business in Belize, the Committee's other major task is marketing their lobster to the rest of the world. The goal is to obtain a contract with a company that agrees to pay a set price for all of a given product the co-op can produce. Usually they are able to negotiate this type of contract for lobster with an American or European restaurant or grocery chain, because of high demand for lobster and Caye Caulker's consistently high-quality product. During the last few years, Red Lobster Inn's of America has purchased the entire lobster production. During some years they have been able to conclude such a contract for the whole conch catch as well. In 1984, three American companies bought the conch production. However, the co-op is usually not able to negotiate this type of agreement for scale fish. Fish are exported mainly to Jamaica through a number of smaller contracts.

The negotiating process begins when competing companies send their bids to the Executive Secretary, who then makes a report to the Managing Committee. After evaluating the bids, the Committee itself negotiates with the bidding companies, whose representatives must fly to Belize and catch a boat to Caye Caulker to present their proposals directly to the Board. The striking image of the suit- and tie-clad marketing representative in the tropical setting of Caye Caulker, trying hard not to get sand in his shoes as he heads for a meeting with seven fishermen, symbolizes for the islanders their co-op's recently won victory over foreign domination.

Influence of the Managing Committee on Caye Caulker

The Managing Committee has considerable power within the organization of the co-op. It also has an important influence on island social and political life. This influence is exercised through the decision to give loans to co-op members. Loans to members are decided on the basis of a man's reputation for hard work and honesty. The loan is paid back from unpaid dividends at the end of the lobster season. The ability to collect a loan therefore depends on two factors; the amount of the catch a member sells to the co-op and his willingness to sell his produce to the co-op. A man who produces too little will not be able to pay back a loan, and a man who sells his produce elsewhere or who sells his produce in the name of his sons rather than his own name will end the year with an outstanding debt. Failure to repay loans is the source of much tension and complaint within the co-op organization. One man on Caye Caulker owes the co-op $20,000 Bz and has made clear his intention not to pay this loan. Meanwhile he filters his produce to the co-op through his sons. The Managing Committee is unwilling to deduct from the sons' income. In the meantime they are trying to get a law passed to force payment of loans, but so far have been unsuccessful. Unpaid loans are cited as a major reason for the folding of the Placencia co-operative and the current problems of the Sarteneja co-operative and the Caribena co-op on San Pedro. The Managing Committee, in determining who gets loans, has a major role in determining the very future of the co-op.

Consequently, the Managing Committee's decisions on loans are not always viewed as impartial by members of the co-op. They must assess the reputation of a man on the basis of personal acquaintance and his record with the co-op. Accusations of favoritism are always present, especially the accusation that members of the Committee regularly loan to themselves, their relatives and friends.

Members of the Managing Committee, because of their position, also have contact and influence with other financial institutions and the Belizean government. This knowledge is often called upon to help individual members. One member of the Managing Committee for several years described his position thus:

> The Committee gives me a lot of experience in running things, and I have a reputation for seeing things through. For example, if someone has a loan from the bank or the Belize Development Office and they can't pay back on time, they come to me and say 'What do I do?' And I say, 'Leave it to me.' I know everybody and I've been around a lot so the next day I

go to the bank and ask them to give him a little more time. I can vouch for him. Lots of people come to me for help.

In addition to an advantage in acquiring a good lobster territory through their families, islanders who have access to loans also have the ability to improve their production through better equipment (lobster traps, skiffs and motors). They also have to work as producers to realize these greater profits. Not all islanders take advantage of these opportunities, but members of the Managing Committee are usually islanders who have consistently done so. Consequently they tend to be better off financially. As one fisherman put it, being on the Committee,

gives them an advantage, but they have to work too. They are the same as anybody else, they just have more money, that's all. They are no more or less honest, but they have more and they protect that.

NOTES

1.   This chapter has been written in collaboration with Laurie Kroshus and has been published in <u>Belizean Studies</u> as "A Social History of Caye Caulker", Vol. 13, No.1, 1985).

2.   Alan K. Craig, <u>Geography of Fishing in British Honduras and Adjacent Coastal Areas</u> (Baton Rouge, Louisiana: Coastal Studies Institute, Louisiana State University, 1966) p. 62.

3.   <u>Ibid</u>, p. 18.

4.   <u>Ibid</u>, pp. 35-36.

5.   <u>Ibid</u>, p. 62.

6.   Glenn D. Godfrey, <u>Ambergris Caye: Paradise with a Past</u> (Belize, Central American: Cubola Productions, 1983) p. 24.

7.   <u>Ibid</u>, p. 30.

8.   <u>Ibid</u>, p. 44.

9.   <u>Ibid</u>, p. 91.

10.   <u>Ibid</u>, p. 91.

11.   <u>Ibid</u>, p. 92.

12.   Susanna Vega, "The Development of Spiny Lobster in Belize, 1920-1977", <u>Belizean Studies</u>, 7, No. 2 (March, 1979), p. 2.

13.   Godfrey, p. 46.

14.   <u>Ibid</u>, p. 46.

15.   <u>Ibid</u>, p. 49.

16.   Vega, p. 2.

17.   Godfrey, p. 45.

18.   Vega, pp. 2-3.

19.   Vega, pp. 2-3 and Godfrey, p. 45.

20.   Godfrey, p. 49.

21.   Vega, p. 3.

22.   Godfrey, p. 51.

23.   Vega, p. 5.

24.   Ibid, p. 5.

25.   William David Setzekorn, Formerly British Honduras: A Profile of the New Nation of Belize (Newark, California: Dumbarton Press, 1975) p. 70.

26.   Godfrey, p. 55.

27.   Ibid, p. 55.

IV

Kinship and Family Structure

There are two important distinctions between people on Caye Caulker: islanders and non-islanders, kin ("family") and non-kin. These distinctions have some important implications. First, islanders have preferential access to land and to membership in the co-op. Second, islanders, through their network of kin have preferential access to lobster territories and to social and economic support. In the absence of ruling families, a rigid class structure and wider forms of social organization, extended families are the main social groups on the island. Islanders espouse an egalitarian ethos and place great importance on an individual's reputation for work and honesty. Within this framework of egalitarian ideals and a lack of wider institutions, some individuals have developed reputations for hard work, loyalty to kin and reliability. Some of these highly regarded men regularly serve on the Managing Committee of the Co-op and their families expand and flourish.

This chapter[1] shall describe the structure of kin relationships and the formation of kin groups based on cognatic descent and family localities in conjunction with "Caribbean" patterns of conjugal ties and "Latin American" patterns of households. First it is necessary to discuss the implications of race and the absence of ruling families based on a color-class hierarchy.

Residence and Ethnicity

The Caribbean area is characterized by a color-class social structure arising from the legacies of mercantile colonialism and the plantation system. Although the plantation system with its hierarchy of masters and slaves never took hold for any length of time in Belize, the country has not escaped the implantation of color-class categories. As in the rest of the New World, race is a basis of social differentiation both in Belize in general and on Caye Caulker.

The five ethnic groups in Belize include Creoles (Afro-European), 31%, Mestizo (Spanish/Amerindian), 33%, Amerindian (Mayan and Kekchi), 19%, Black Caribs (Afro-Indian), 11%, and German Mennonites, 4%. In contrast to Jamaica, Haiti, and Barbados which are 90% African and the Dominican Republic, Cuba, and Puerto Rico which are 70% to 80% white or Mestizo, Belize as a whole is not clearly dominated by one color-class or ethnic category[2]. However, ethnic groups are not spread evenly in Belize and each area, city, or region is composed predominantly of one ethnic group or another.

On Caye Caulker, the dominant category is Mestizo, which is locally referred to as Spanish. There is only one family of 'African' descent that is considered native to the island. A number of mainland Creoles and a few Black Caribs rent houses on the island on a semipermanent basis. Their residence depends partly on the availability of work. Caribs, for example, have often been hired to clear the airstrip. Other government jobs (policeman and nurse) are filled by Creoles, although the government tries to provide one Spanish policeman and one Creole policeman on the island. There are no Amerindians on Caye Caulker although various people speak of their 'Mayan heritage' with pride.

It is important to note that color is not the dominant means of identification on Caye Caulker. In most contexts, the most important distinction is islander in contrast to a nonislander. It is interesting that apart from the English word islander, which is in general use on Caye Caulker, there are many phrases such as 'I belong to Caye Caulker' that draw the distinction between insider and outsider. In Spanish, the term used is _Jicaqueño_, which means a person from Caye Caulker[3].

Since most families viewed as islanders are also Spanish, residence contains an implied ethnic designation. In conversation, reference to race may be used mainly to identify an islander who is not Spanish. Furthermore, a non-islander also can be identified by place of origin rather than the more controversial racial designation. Thus, the term "Belizean" usually refers to both someone from Belize City as well as a Creole ethnic identity. San Pedrano refers to people from San Pedro on Ambergris Caye, who also are mostly Spanish. People from places in Belize other than Caye Caulker are usually identified by place as in 'He's a Sarteneja fisherman' or 'He's from Corozal' rather than by ethnicity or race.

Although race is relevant as a means of social identification (on Caye Caulker), it is not the basis of a local socioeconomic hierarchy. Two factors contribute to this lack of a local color-class hierarchy. First, the island is relatively undifferentiated racially; it is virtually dominated by one ethnic group, the Spanish. Second, the most important economic advantages and the primary access to status derive from being an islander, a Jicaqueño. These status and economic advantages are based on membership in a kin group, which is the basis for access to a lobster territory, and preferential access to land for residence. The rest of this chapter is a discussion of these kinship-related issues, beginning with the link between cognatic descent and residence on Caye Caulker.

Cognatic Descent

According to Raymond T. Smith[4], Caribbean kinship systems are typified by ego-focused, cognatic, noncorporate kindred organization. Caye Caulker is no exception. People on Caye Caulker trace descent cognatically (through father and mother) using the same kin terms that are used in English. As in many cognatic systems, for practical purposes, descent is rarely traced beyond the second cousin. People who can trace descent to each other up to second cousin must be considered kin and are referred to as 'family.' People who can trace a kinship relationship beyond second cousin may choose to consider themselves kin, particularly when personal ties develop between the two individuals. People on Caye Caulker belong to loosely formed cognatic kin groups that are lumped together under a family surname. Residence is an important factor in cementing kinship ties. People who leave the island, usually to immigrate to the United States, usually give up a claim to a cognatic kin group

and maintain ties only with members of their immediate
family.

Most important social ties on Caye Caulker are based
on kinship. The community is composed of a small number
of cognatic kin groups who are related to each other
through marriage. The largest kin groups living on Caye
Caulker are known by the surnames Barones, Williams,
Martin, and Lenos. In addition, there are several other
smaller kin groups on the island. People from these
families have married with the larger kin groups and often
are associated very closely with them. For example, the
Cortez extended families are linked with the Williams
family, and several Morenos have intermarried with
Martins. Complicated relationships ensue because of the
many marriages between few families. Some claim,
jokingly, that they are related to nearly everyone on the
island but are not sure how. The easiest way to
understand the relationships is to take account of two
variables: the surname of the person and the location of
the person's residence or household.

Surnames

The acquisition of a surname is generally
patrilineal but not rigidly so. Most children take their
father's last name (whether he was married to their mother
or not), although they may and sometimes do take their
mother's name if they choose. Women also generally take
their husband's last name at marriage. Although the use
of surnames may be fluid, changing to fit the
circumstances, often knowing a person's last name will
automatically give an indication of group membership and
residence. For instance, four Martin brothers live near
one another in the Martin family locale. A fifth brother
lives in Belize City temporarily, while his children are
in secondary school, but he keeps his house in the family
locality until he can move back there. Several other
relatives, who are counted as part of the Martin kin group
but have different surnames, live in the same general
area.

Sometimes the last name of a person fails to reveal
the tie to a major kin group. In this case it is
important to determine where the person lives and through
which kin tie he or she obtained land to build a house.
For example, three of the Martin sisters also live in the
Martin family locale with their husband and children. One
sister married a Hernandez, but as they remained on Martin

land, they and their children are considered part of that extended family. When one of their daughters married a Williams, he was also accepted as part of the Martin family. He worked in the bar run by his wife's uncle and went fishing with the men in the Martin family. When he and his wife separated, and he began living with a girl from another family, he no longer was considered part of the Martin kin group.

Family Localities

Identification with a family name, participation in a family support network, and acquisition of land on Caye Caulker are all closely connected. The large kin groups on Caye Caulker are situated in specific areas of the island. These areas or localities are a spatial arena for the family network. Family members visit each other, borrow from each other, and share economic and social support within a specific area of the village. Furthermore, families in one locale do not usually visit other parts of the island. Messages may be sent by children to other areas, but for the most part people keep within their own family site. One result of this lack of movement around the island is that individual islanders often have more contact with Belize City than they do with other parts of the island. One day Edith Moreno, a 15 year old who has lived on Caye Caulker all her life and attended school in Belize City, reluctantly took a walk with me to the southern end of the island. As we left her family locale she became nervous and informed me that she had not been to 'Shirley's house,' some 200 yards from her own, since she was twelve.

This limited movement around the island is possible because the larger family localities are fairly self-sufficient. Each locality has a main pier, shared by the kin who live in that area. In this way even inland houses have access to the sea, a place to dock their skiff and to clean their catch. The localities of the larger kin groups also have a dry goods store run by one of the families in the kin group. Someone in the locale may bake bread or make coconut oil which family members (and others too) can buy. People in family localities often rely on reciprocal exchange rather than cash. If they need to borrow tools or equipment, or require help with building or transporting, they may give a loaf of bread, a bottle of rum, or some fish in return. People also help each other without payment. For example, they may get together

Map 5

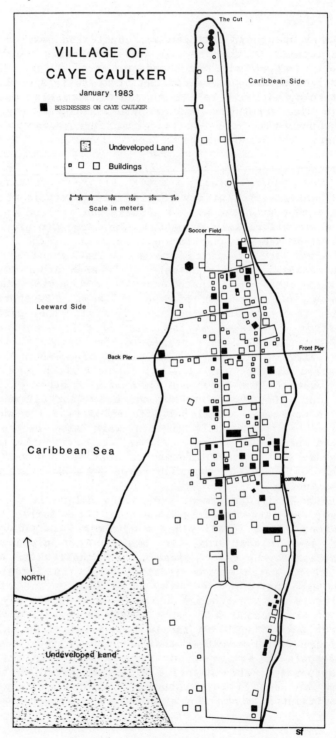

VILLAGE OF
CAYE CAULKER

January 1983

■ BUSINESSES ON CAYE CAULKER

Undeveloped Land

▫ ◻ ◻ Buildings

0 25 50   100   150   200   250
Scale in meters

The Cut

Caribbean Side

Soccer Field

Leeward Side

Back Pier

Front Pier

Caribbean Sea

cemetery

↑
NORTH

Undeveloped Land

Sf

to haul a boat, and then share a bottle of rum under a coconut tree. Or they may allow kin to collect breadfruit and sell them without any expectations of return. Each family locale also has one or more hotels, rental houses, restaurants, bars, or bakeries for the tourist trade. Map 5 shows that businesses are well distributed throughout the island with each locale supporting most necessary services. Thus, no one has to leave a locale to buy what is needed. Consequently, for the most part, family members do not stray too far from their area. Only on rare occasions and usually for specific reasons, does one find a Barones at the southern end of the island or a Martin at the northern end.

There are eight main family localities on Caye Caulker. From north to south, these are the Barones, Alameda, Jimenez, Santos, Hernandez, Martin, Lenos, and Williams families. The Barones and Martin families have the largest localities, but in all cases, although the localities are relatively self-sufficient areas where families work and live, there is still a fair amount of overlapping with families in other localities on the island.

The Barones locality (Map 6), for example, consists of the households of John, Sr., and his grown children, John, Jr., Maria Brown, and Mike. In each of these households live large numbers of children from whom other households have developed. Maria's daughter and the local school teacher, is married to Richard Moreno, and they have three children. John, Jr., and Eve have six children. One of these children, Lorilei, lives nearby with her husband, Charles Williams. In addition, John has an adult son who lives with Miss Priscilla. Mike and his wife have seven grown children; three are married. One married daughter lives with her husband and son in her father's house and runs the pastry shop in front. His wife's mother lives next door with her grown son. In addition, there are two hotels, a liquor store, a dry goods store, and four rent houses. Two Barones households serve meals in the evening to tourists.

How do we account for the formation of these family localities? First, it is important to note that although the availability of land for building a house is limited, in the past when subsistence fishing was the only source of income, land was inexpensive. At this time families purchased land very cheaply and passed it on to their descendants. New households could thus be established with additional purchases adjacent to kin localities. In

Map 6

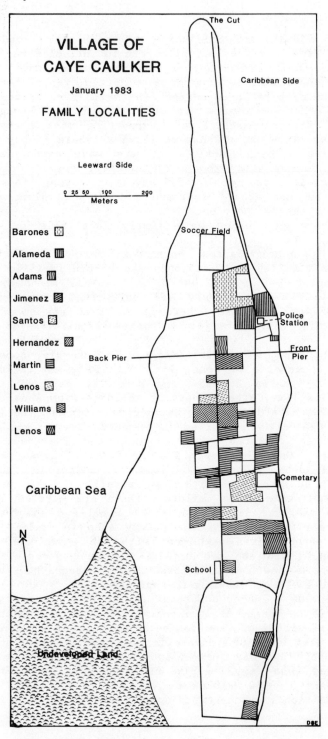

VILLAGE OF
CAYE CAULKER

January 1983

FAMILY LOCALITIES

The Cut

Caribbean Side

Leeward Side

0 25 50   100   200
       Meters

Barones
Alameda
Adams
Jimenez
Santos
Hernandez
Martin
Lenos
Williams
Lenos

Soccer Field

Police
Station

Back Pier

Front
Pier

Cemetary

Caribbean Sea

N

School

Undeveloped Land

the past ten years this easy access to land has changed on Caye Caulker. Now that commercial fishing is profitable and tourism is a source of income, the village is growing, and land has become very expensive and scarce. People are concerned with keeping the land in their families and are careful not to allow it to be sold to foreigners. There are now several ways that the land is acquired. It may be inherited, purchased from kin, or drawn by lottery at the new site.

Inherited

A common way land has been obtained is through inheritance. Eduardo and Ramon Lenos' grandfather owned a large section of Caye Caulker in the middle of the village (see Map 6). He transferred the title of several plots to Edwardo and Ramon. Their sister did not inherit land from her grandfather; but her husband was able to buy his land nearby from another big landowner. Much of the Barones land was also inherited through Mike's wife Polli from her father Pablo Santos, Sr. There is pressure to keep land in the family. "Families try to live together if they can. My uncle was going to sell his land, but my father wanted to keep it in the family so he bought it. Then he distributed it to his kids. All ten of the Sanchez kids inherited land on the island. They still own their lots although four live in Belize City and five in the U.S. Nobody sells land. We would rather pass it along to family."

Purchase from Kin

When land is purchased, people try to buy a piece close to their kin, and people who wish to sell land are expected to sell to their kin. Selling land to nonkin is viewed as somewhat unscrupulous. There is some feeling that kin have a right to choice of the land, and the owner does not have the right to sell to nonkin. There is no stigma attached to buying or selling land which is not close to one's family locale.

For example, the Martin locality began with one corner lot owned by the father. Gradually he bought land around this lot from someone who lived in Belize City and lost interest in it. Then Mr. Martin distributed the land among his children, including his daughters. But some of his children bought pieces nearby.

The New Site

Because of the demand for lots to build houses, the Belizean government has purchased a large tract of land near the cut at the north end of the island (see Map 4). Both islanders and other Belizeans who are over 18 and do not already have land can apply for lots, but islanders have first preference. Applicants are screened by the land committee, which is made up of members of the village council. If they are approved, they participate in a raffle to draw a lot. Then the person is allowed to buy the lot for a nominal amount paid each year for 20 years. A condition of purchase is that U.S.$2,500 of improvements must be made on the lot in two years, or the land is forfeited. There are reported to be 64 lots in the new site. A large number have been allocated and must have improvements (houses) erected by May 1984 or be forfeited. The April 1984 payment of shares at the co-op initiated a flurry of building activity at the new site.

The building at the new site is significant because it is becoming a new community populated mainly by young single men and women and new families. Because of the lottery system the location of the lots is random, and the formation of family localities similar to the older part of the village is not taking place. However, when clear ownership of land is obtained, and land begins to change hands, it is possible that family localities may emerge.

Access to land has been a major factor in the formation of kin group localities. Though new areas are developing on Caye Caulker -- in Marcial town, where foreigners have bought land, and at the new site -- no major change in the localities has taken place. We have seen that each locality is formed around a group of siblings and their descendants. We can now examine the structure of domestic groups within a locality and the mating patterns that produce those domestic groups.

Sexual Relationships

There is a direct connection between sexual relationships, mating patterns, and the composition of the domestic group. An understanding of the characteristics of sexual relationships on Caye Caulker is basic to understanding mating patterns, household composition, and kinship ties in general.

Sexual relationships on Caye Caulker conform to the general pattern of sexual mores found in the Caribbean area and are not similar to rules of sexual behavior found in the rest of Central America. Generally in Latin America the assumption is that sex is normal for men but that women must control themselves and men both before and after marriage. Virginity in women is highly valued, and a woman's personal honor, as well as that of her family and especially of her men folk, is based on her virginity before marriage and chastity after marriage. The ideal prototype woman in Latin America is the Virgin Mary, who remains pure but becomes a mother nonetheless. Men enjoy sexual freedom, but have the responsibility to oversee the chastity of the women of their family. At the same time, they seek to undermine the chastity of women of other families in order to prove their ability to make sexual conquests[5].

The Caribbean area generally and Caye Caulker in particular present a very different view of sexual relations. Sex is considered normal; both men and women are assumed to have sexual desire and are expected to satisfy the desire sometime after age 15 or 16. Personal and family honor are not really affected by loss of virginity. Marriage is valued, but consensual unions are the norm.

The Development of Conjugal Ties

Mating patterns on Caye Caulker are very similar to those found in the Caribbean area in general. The three kinds of unions, for example, found in Barbados and in Belize in general, are also prevalent on Caye Caulker.[6] These are Christian marriage, consensual unions, and visiting relationships. Consensual unions are common-law unions where partners live in the same household, and visiting relationships are conjugal relationships where partners live in different households. The formation of a conjugal relationship begins with a visiting relationship, although a person may develop visiting relationships throughout his or her lifetime. Visiting relationships are the least stable of the three kinds of unions.

On the island, visiting is very subtle and low key. Adolescents become interested in the opposite sex from about age 12 and express this interest to their friends. Boys begin to hang out in front of a girl's house or walk back and forth in front of her house. If she is interested she will come outside and talk with him. Young people may be seen standing on the sand lanes talking in the evenings or when school is just out. Parents are watchful of their daughters until they are about 18 and discourage a relationship that becomes too serious. Many of the boys and girls go to Belize City for their secondary education. The school in Belize City is segregated by sex and in order to meet girls, boys wait outside the entrance to the girls' schools until classes are over for the day. When the girls come out of class, they stand around and talk to each other. After meeting a couple of times, the boy might walk the girl home from school. Then they might begin to go out on a Saturday or Friday night to a movie, dance, or to get something to eat. On Caye Caulker, however, this kind of courtship is not possible. The only place to go is a bar. Couples never go to these places, although boys may go with other boys for a drink. Also on Caye Caulker there is only a small number of young people between 12 and 18 because they must go to Belize City to complete their education. Only those who decide not to continue with school are on the island.

Young people begin to form sexual relationships between ages 15 and 17. Popular places for 'fooling around' are anchored skiffs on the reef, in the mangrove swamps, in boats drawn up on the beach, and at the end of the pier at night. An anchored and apparently empty skiff at the reef is a signal to passing boats to keep their distance and give the couple privacy. At night if a radio is playing at the end of the pier, which is invisible in the dark, the expectation is that one not walk out to the end of the pier. In the last few years, since foreigners are not so aware of these rules, the pier has become a less popular place for trysts.

When a girl has a child, there is pressure for the boy to recognize the child as his. Men are usually eager to recognize the child and take responsibility for contributing to the child's support. Once a child is born, the visiting relationship usually becomes more established. There may also be pressure to change the union to a consensual union. Partly this move depends upon the ages of the couple, whether the boy is able to support the girl, and whether they can find a place to live (either by renting a house from a relative or by building one at the cut). If they do not move in together, it is likely that the relationship will end. The birth of a child does not necessarily create a stable union. One young man, for example, turned a visiting relationship into a consensual union when the girl had his child, but the relationship only lasted 9 months because

she moved out and formed a visiting relationship with
another man. The father of the child continued to provide
financial assistance although he only had sporadic contact
with mother and child.

A woman's second pregnancy, whether by the father of
the first child or by another, usually results in the
formation of a consensual union or marriage. With the
need to support two children, a woman is under greater
pressure to establish a more stable relationship. The
families of both the woman and the man will also be
pressuring them to form a domestic unit with a stable
income. Although both man and woman can always live with
their parents, personal and economic independence is
highly valued, and the tendency is for them to have their
own household as soon as possible.

On Caye Caulker, mating patterns include the three
kinds of unions described for Creole populations in
Belize, but the development pattern of these unions shows
some important differences. Although visiting is an early
form of courtship and mating, it is also a relationship
that can occur any time throughout a person's life
regardless of any other relationship. A man or woman
living in a consensual union or marriage may also
undertake a visiting relationship that will not develop
into a household (although there have been cases of people
leaving a consensual union because of a visiting
relationship). These relationships may produce children
who are usually incorporated into the woman's household.

Consensual unions are very common and accepted, but
it is the relationship between consensual unions and
Christian marriage that is most interesting on Caye
Caulker. Christian marriage carries prestige but is not a
requirement for a socially acceptable union. The most
common developmental cycle for households on Caye Caulker
seems to be to start with a Christian marriage early in
life. This marriage may end in separation, in which case
the person moves on to a consensual union that is more
long term and stable than the early marriage. Several
families on Caye Caulker have stable households based on a
consensual union that has followed a brief and
unsuccessful early marriage. In one case a man recently
married his common-law wife, after their grown children
had left home, because he realized that he could annul an
early unsuccessful marriage. In another case an early
Christian marriage dissolved only after the birth of five
children. The man began a consensual union (after a
visiting relationship of some years during his marriage)

with a woman. This union resulted in the formation of
another household and produced a large family. In the
meantime, he had other visiting relationships. The wife
kept her own house and the five children of her marriage;
she had two more children from visiting relationships.
Finally, when the wife died in old age, the husband
married the foreigner with whom he had formed a third
consensual union. Christian marriage appears to happen
either early in life or late in life. Many households and
families are formed on the basis of a consensual union
that occurs sometime in between.

Norman Ashcraft's[7] description of mating patterns and
the development of conjugal ties for Creoles in rural
Belize has striking parallels to the pattern found on Caye
Caulker. In both the Creole rural population and on Caye
Caulker, economic differences are slight, and there is a
lack of color-class hierarchy. Furthermore, monogamous
unions are the rule, new households are established by
conjugal couples, and nuclear family households prevail.
There are some important differences, however, between the
rural Creoles and the Spanish islanders. Ashcraft
describes Creole kin bonds as "amorphous" and they vary
from strong to weak, whereas the household is the "one
unit demonstrating some sign of structural
relationships."[8] As we have seen, on Caye Caulker, kin
bonds are strong and are structured into kin groups that
have a specific locale in the village and a network of
relationships based on mutual obligations, exchange, and
support. All of these factors on Caye Caulker indicate a
stronger kinship orientation than among Creoles in Belize.
Many of these differences may be related to the Mestizo
cultural background of the islanders. A more important
factor is the necessity to acquire land from kin and keep
kinship ties strong or move off the island for lack of a
place to live.

The connection between the mating system in the
Caribbean and the variety of domestic groups formed
therein has been dealt with extensively in the literature.
Nancy Gonzalez,[9] for example, focuses primarily on the
distinction between family (kinship ties) and households
(domestic groups) and argues that there is no necessary
connection between kinship relationships and members of a
household. Whereas families tend to be connected through
a conjugal relationship, households may or may not contain
such a kin tie. This situation is not generally the case
on Caye Caulker where Caribbean mating patterns have still
resulted in the formation of households based on a

conjugal unit and the nuclear family. Men on Caye Caulker generally have sufficient economic security to form a relationship with a woman that will lead to the establishment of a new household. Households headed by women are economically far more unstable because women lack access to a means of economic support. Women-headed households are generally lacking in fishing communities where the division of labor requires both genders. Although households do dissolve and new ones form, they almost always are formed on the basis of a conjugal relationship and develop into nuclear families. Extended family members and young single people usually have their own households, although these households are always operating in close cooperation with a kin locality and the kin group living there. Single people, young or old, share household duties, food preparation, washing clothes, and exchange of services, with households composed of conjugal units.

Another pattern of recent development on Caye Caulker is the formation of households based on the conjugal relationship between an island man and a foreign woman. Contrary to the Caribbean pattern that grew out of the plantation system where a higher status white man formed a union with a lower status (black) slave mistress, on Caye Caulker the reverse is true.[10] Island men are forming unions with foreign (white) women. Sometimes these unions produce children, but they are generally unstable. Frequently a woman stays only long enough for the man to support her and the child for one year, when she returns to her country with the baby. Although there are a few cases of longer relationships and some that involve marriage, the great majority of these relationships are short-lived. On the other hand, foreign women past childbearing age are more likely to enter into long term relationships with island men and settle more permanently on Caye Caulker.

It is interesting to note that island women do not readily seek foreign men as husbands or mates. When they do marry a foreigner, they have little chance of remaining on the island. Foreign men are not encouraged to work at fishing and tourism since they are viewed as competition for the islanders. In all cases where island women married Canadians or Americans, they eventually emmigrated to those countries. At one time two such cases were living on Caye Caulker. One of the men became a member of the Co-op and took tourists to the reef, and the other ran a store, but both have since left. One of the men remarked that without the support of family ties, it is very difficult to earn a living on the island.

Island women who wish to remain on Caye Caulker therefore must find a mate from among the island men who are becoming fishermen or marry a Belizean or Central American migrant who can work along with her family. There are several such cases. Jessica Barones has married a Salvadoran. Her husband started fishing with her relatives and now has his own lobster traps and territory. Jessica, who runs a pastry shop in front of her father's house, is also aided by her husband in the business. Not only does he bring her lobster for her lobster quiche that appears every day at 2:30 pm, but he also squeezes the oranges for the bottles of fresh orange juice she sells. Emilio Moreno's daughter also married a Belizean who is now helping Emilio with boat runs from Belize City to Caye Caulker and has begun fishing with his wife's brother.

Conclusions

The main categories of people on Caye Caulker are islanders (Jicaqueños) and nonislanders, kin and nonkin. Islanders have many advantages over nonislanders. The islanders are members of a cognatic kin group. Through kin they obtain preferential access to land in kin localities. Members of a kin group also rely on each other for social and economic support: they exchange goods and services, and they form close, supportive personal ties. On Caye Caulker the household is part of and is supported by a larger residential unit, the kin locality. Households within kin localities are established on the basis of a conjugal relationship that produces a nuclear family. This 'Latin American' pattern of household structure exists in conjunction with characteristic 'Caribbean' patterns of sexual relationships and mating.

NOTES

1.   This chapter has been published in <u>Belizean
Studies</u>, Vol. 13, Nos. 5 & 6, Dec. 1985. Laurie Kroshus
and Janet Fuller provided some data for the article;
however, I am solely responsible for the writing and
conclusions.

2.   Population Census of the Commonwealth
Caribbean, 1970 (Univ. of the West Indies, Census Research
Programme).

3.   In Spanish, Caye Caulker is called Cayo
Jicaco.   According to Leo Bradley,"Glimpses of our
History" (Oct. 1962, Vol. 4A), <u>jicaco</u> refers to the coco
plum which grows in abundance on Caye Caulker. Presumably
Caye Caulker is an English alliteration of Cayo Jicaco
(National Collection, Bliss Inst., Belize City).

4.   Smith, Raymond T. "The Family and the Modern
World System: Some Observations from the Caribbean,"
<u>Journal of Family History</u>, Vol. 3, No. 4, Winter, 1978.

5.   This norm is translated into practice more
among the middle classes than upper or lower classes.
However, the norm, if not the practice, is espoused by all
classes. (See Lewis, Oscar, <u>The Children of Sanchez</u>,
Vintage Books, 1963.

6.   Ashcraft, Norman, "Some Aspects of Domestic
Organization in British Honduras" in <u>The Family in the
Caribbean</u>, Stanford N. Gerber, ed., University of Puerto
Rico: Institute of Caribbean Studies, 1968 (pages63-73);
and Sutton, Constance and Makiesky-Barrow, Susan, "Social
Inequality and Sexual Status in Barbados" in <u>The Black
Woman Cross-Culturally</u>, Filomina Chioma Steady, ed.,
Cambridge, Mass.: Schenkman Publishing Co., 1981 (pages
483-485).

7.   <u>Ibid</u>., Ashcraft.

8.   <u>Ibid</u>., page 64.

9.   Gonzalez, Nancie Solien, "Household and Family
in the Caribbean: Some Definitions and Concepts," in <u>The
Black Woman Cross-Culturally</u>, Filomina Chioma Steady, ed.,
Cambridge, Mass.: Schenkman Publishing Co., 1981.

86

10. See Martinez-Alier, Verena, _Marriage, Class and Color in Nineteenth Century Cuba. A Study of Racial Attitudes and Sexual Values in a Slave Society_. London: Cambridge University Press, 1974.

V

Domestic Social Relationships

The domestic group on Caye Caulker is a household which contains a nuclear family: a man and woman living in a conjugal relationship, their own children and any children from previous conjugal relationships. Within the domestic group there is a clear but not a strict division of labor for women, men, and children. Most island activities can be classified according to the appropriate gender and age, but in particular circumstances there is acceptance of a certain amount of crossing over into roles other than the most appropriate. Responsibilities are viewed as complementary, with each person contributing to the functioning of the household as a whole.

In the household a man is expected to provide financially for his wife and children. On Caye Caulker men provide this support primarily through fishing. Fishing is men's work and being a fisherman is a primary identity for a man. Not all men take to the fisherman's life. By the time a boy is ready to enter secondary school in Belize City, he usually knows if he is interested in returning to become a fisherman. Some do not return. For example, Sally Martin has a son in the United States who is training to be an electrician. Most parents on Caye Caulker understand and accept the idea that not all young boys want to be fishermen. They encourage these sons to continue with their education and to compete for other jobs. On the other hand, boys who want to fish often do not continue their schooling and begin to earn a living by the time they are 13. Several young men on the island have taken this route and were economically self-sufficient by the time they were 15.

In addition to fishing, men may establish tourist-related businesses, such as a bar, shop or restaurant. They also take tourists to the reef, to Belize City, and to San Pedro, handle tourist needs in a hotel, and take responsibility for building hotel, restaurant, and shop facilities. Some men, who in the past were full-time fishermen, have retired and turned to tourism. Emilio Moreno, who built the first hotel in 1970, claims to be the first fisherman on Caye Caulker to retire and work only at tourism. Bob Rodriguez and his family also run a combination hotel, bar, 'cinema,' and restaurant that is one of the few businesses on Caye Caulker that is always open.

A few men are also known for their ability as boat builders or carpenters. The Williams family, for instance, has a reputation for producing good carpenters and boat builders. Peter Williams and his son are master boat builders and are highly regarded for this work. Two other sons are also carpenters and are sought by foreigners wanting a house built. All four men have also worked as fishermen all their lives.

Men are responsible for all activities related to fishing, boats, motors, and building. They run and repair boat motors, they haul up, repair, and paint boats, sew and repair sails, and make and repair all fishing equipment (lobster traps, nets, lines, etc.). They will also build houses and maintain them. Men and boys also clear yards of weeds and haul garbage to the back of the island.

Men will also do jobs that are generally considered women's work: cooking, washing, and cleaning without hesitation when circumstances dictate, that is, when there is no woman to do them. For example, when Miss Priscilla went to the United States last year, her husband took over the restaurant and became the cook in the evenings after a day's fishing. However, eventually men seek a woman to perform those tasks. One job that island men do not normally take on is the entire responsibility for raising children.

Women may line fish at times, learn to spot lobster traps, or clean the inside of a boat, but they do not become fishermen. Although two women joined the co-op at its inception, none belong now, and no woman makes a living through fishing. One man, whose son has no interest in fishing, commented on his daughter who, in his opinion, is a natural in the water and on boats:

> She loves to work with me when I go out. She handles the sails and loves to fish. Too bad she can never make a living from fishing. She's a girl.

A number of men's jobs take place at home and in the kin locality. Building lobster traps, mending nets, and building or repairing houses can be done close to home, and men are often seen working outside the house on various projects. However, part of their work such as fishing, selling produce at the co-op, or buying supplies in Belize City does require them to go beyond the kin locality. Working outside in public puts men in daily contact with one another, and during their leisure time they may socialize in public places such as the lanes, bars, and the main docks. A fisherman often spends his mornings at sea, the afternoons at home working on a project, and the evenings socializing with other men.

In contrast, a woman's sphere of activity is domestic and focuses on the kin locality. The woman is responsible for taking care of her children, for preparing the family's meals, washing clothes, cleaning the house and yard, and looking after the family's religious and educational interests. The greater part of each day is taken up with domestic chores that revolve around the home. Women have less time than men to visit friends and relatives. Occasionally women can be seen walking their children to school or to church. They are rarely seen standing in their yards visiting with neighbors, running errands, or even walking to the house next door. Women do not usually swim at the cut or off the end of the pier, though they do go out in boats with their fathers or husbands.

On Caye Caulker women are generally less visible than men because they stay in their homes. For example, one day a house caught fire and there was a rapid blaze that could be seen from one end of the island to the other. Rumors spread quickly that a baby had been left in the house while the mother was batheing in the sea. People came running from all over only to discover that the baby was safe and that nothing could be done for the house, which burned to the ground, taking three coconut trees with it. For a brief moment, over one hundred women had emerged from their houses to see the fire. One foreigner, who at the time had lived on Caye Caulker for five years, commented:

> At the time of the fire, I saw women I had never seen before and have never seen since. I have never seen that many women on Caye Caulker in one place at one time. I can't figure out where they all came from. Some of the women I knew well, but I had never seen them outside their houses.

On Caye Caulker the words woman and mother are used interchangeably. A girl becomes a woman when she becomes a mother. Being a mother is a primary role for women and defines women in general. Women are expected to have an active sexuality and are not sexually controlled by men. Although women are expected to form stable unions and have children, the status of a family is not dependent on the sexual purity of its women. Being a mother is not viewed as diminishing a woman's sexuality. It is not unusual for girls and women (mothers) to have visiting relationships; however, while for men a visiting relationship in addition to a consensual union is viewed as the norm, for women it is somewhat less acceptable.

Men and women have clear and separate duties in relation to their families. Men are expected to provide financially for their conjugal partner and any children they produce. Women are expected to care for their children, cook, and perform household duties. In either case, those who fail in these regards are shirking their duties. Several years ago, a 40-year-old mother of ten children ran off with a 19-year-old boy leaving all her children with their father when the youngest was still an infant. The consensus of island gossip was that although going away with a 19-year-old was not particularly surprising, they were shocked that she would leave her children behind.

Most women on Caye Caulker expect to become wives and mothers as adults and to perform traditional roles. An example of a traditional wife and mother is Mariana Sanchez. Mariana lives in one of two cement houses on the island with Agosto, her husband of 15 years, and their four children: Ruby, a 15-year-old daughter who lives in Belize City with Mariana's sister while attending high school; 11-year-old Alberto, who is finishing school on Caye Caulker; Juanito, who is three; and the baby, Sara.

Mariana's daily routine supports her assertion that "We women live in the kitchen." She gets up in the morning while her neighbors are rising to their early morning chores of husking coconuts, raking the sand in their yards, and wheeling tanks of gas down to the pier. She makes breakfast, perhaps panadas - shark-meat pastries -- for Juanito to take to Agosto when he trots over to the co-op to visit his father. Unlike other mothers, she often walks Alberto to school in the morning.

Mariana then cleans the house and washes clothes every other day in a washing machine with a wringer she bought from an American who brings appliances whenever he comes to Caye Caulker. Because she hangs the clothes on a line to dry, they may remain there for days if a sudden downpour catches them. Although islanders may wear a piece of clothing for several consecutive days, dirty clothes for five people, including an infant, accumulate quickly.

The biggest meal on Caye Caulker is the noon meal, for which Agosto returns to eat with Mariana and the children by 12:30. After the dishes are washed, Mariana has a period of several hours before supper which she spends in one of various ways: she either goes back to her laundry, sews, or bakes Creole bread. Juanito and Sara have a nap, and sometimes she takes one, too.

Evening begins around 2:00 on Caye Caulker, and soon after that is a good time to leave the house for awhile. The same American who brought the washing machine also recently brought her a stroller, which makes the promenade easier. On Tuesday, she goes to check for mail at the "store" near the school. Sometimes she goes to the co-op to sit and talk with her husband and pick up the fish she will cook for dinner.

Mariana begins to cook supper, often lobster and rice, about 6:00 and the family eats at 7:00. Sometimes they watch the news from Florida on the TV they acquired in the last year, although the reception is often very poor. After dinner, Mariana takes the children to the Assembly of God church. When she comes home at 9:00 it is time for bed. "Everybody stays home at night. After a strenuous day on the water, the men go to bed because they are tired." Agosto goes out to Martin's bar for a beer only on weekends.

Once a month Mariana skiffs into Belize City to shop. She goes to one supermarket for everything she needs. Between these trips she buys vegetables and meat in the stores nearby. When she is in Belize City, she stays one or two nights with her sister where her daughter is staying while attending school. Agosto also buys groceries when he has to make a trip to Belize City.

Mariana has undertaken many things to bring money into the home, but she has had to discontinue most of them because "taking care of the children is my duty." For two years she taught in the school. When she first began to teach school, her family needed the money, and she enjoyed the work. But problems soon arose.

> Agosto wants his food on time. I expected him to take over some of the work, but he wanted to finish his boats. I never asked him for help. If he gets fish at the co-op, he might cook it, but he thinks that is women's work. The only time he took over the housework, sweeping sand from the floor and doing the laundry, was when I was ill for three days. That's why he got married - not to do those things.

Agosto felt that Mariana did not have enough time on weekends to do all the housework and finally said, "I have enough money, you don't have to work." Several years ago she started a kindergarten in her house for 18 children of islanders and foreigners, then she made bread for awhile, but now she only tutors one child after school and does laundry for visiting tourists. The money she earns is hers. "Sometimes I'll put some money aside, but then we'll need it."

Mariana never goes out to the reef, but she likes to fish off the dock near the co-op. On Sundays, the family walks together to the cut to go swimming or perhaps take a boat ride to nearby Caye Chapel. Like most islanders, her favorite activity is visiting family members, but it is not often that she can do so. Mariana visits her best friend only twice a month because she lives too far away, a 7 to 8 minute walk. On rare occasions she also visits the pastor's wife, Alberto's teacher, her sisters and the ice cream shop. Although her father lives on the island, she does not see him often. The households of her kin, the Santos family, are more physically separated from one another than most other families.

Mariana believes that women do not leave their family areas because 'the women aren't trusted by the men. They want us to stay home.' She once saw a plaque in Martin's bar which said: "Woman was made from the rib of man. She was not made from his head to top him, nor from his feet to be trampled on. She was made from his side to be loved and protected." She felt this was a good summary of how a relationship between a man and a woman should be. She thinks that on Caye Caulker the strength of the woman is in the home. "A woman should be in the home to cook and take care of her home, children, and husband cheerfully."

Mariana is responsible for most of the disciplining of the children. She believes that a strong spanking is much more effective than keeping them inside for a day. She is also concerned with the family's religious interests. "On Caye Caulker, the father isn't that much interested in church. They have it made. They don't need church." At church, she is president of the women's group. She is also the secretary for the Sunday School and teaches the boys' classes. To raise funds for the church, she organized a bake sale. In her home she prays together with her children and sometimes borrows an American's cassette recorder to play Christian tapes. Once a week or so she fasts for a day to add meaning to her prayers, although she continues to cook and serve meals to her family.

Mariana is also responsible for dealing with the children's education. When Alberto comes home from school, he shows her a test or worksheet for the day. She helps him with his homework and makes sure he gets it done. She feels that the encouragement of a parent is important even if only to make sure the child gets to school, and to get the year's supply of textbooks in Belize City. The police only rarely enforce the truancy law so it is up to the parents to encourage children to go to school.

Tourism and Changes in Women's Economic Position

Ten years ago the only viable source of income for women on the island came from the few teaching jobs at the local primary school. These jobs have always gone to recent graduates from college, girls who return to the island and teach until they have families of their own. Women who were widowed or abandoned by a husband could make coconut oil and bake bread, but the income from these tasks was meager, and these women depended heavily on relatives to help them financially until they could establish another union with a man. Basically, a woman-headed household has not been a viable unit on Caye

Caulker since even the support of a large group of relatives can provide only limited financial support. One women remarked:

> There are virtually no single women on the island who live without a man, not even living with their own grown children. Likewise, a widower usually seeks another woman to share his space and fulfill his needs.

The division of labor and the complementarity of men and women's responsibilities in the domestic group make the conjugal unit an important part of every household.

Today there has been a major shift in economic opportunities for women on Caye Caulker. During the last ten years, tourism has created the possibility of a higher income for women, in particular, women with an established restaurant, hotel, or shop. The creation of a tourist business from the household does not change the roles the women and men perform. Men build a hotel or shop onto the house, and women cook and clean for the tourists. Nevertheless, it does present an income change that could have important future consequences. Women are for the first time getting a cash income from this work. Although the possibility of economic independence for women is likely to have an impact on general relations between men and women, the immediate impact is more specific. First, by working as part of their family's business, more girls will be able to stay on the island. When they form their own household, they can continue to bring in an income and contribute to the support of their children. Second, a household can now have a more varied means of support without depending totally on fishing. When income from fishing is low, women sell coconut pies and garnaches (fried tortilla covered with refried beans and hot peppers) from their homes and can bring in a much needed supplemental income. Third, some women now run a regular business, a restaurant or hotel that is open the year round. Most depend on their partner's help in these endeavors, and some run the business jointly; however, most men continue to fish and operate a lobster territory, working the tourist trade only during slack fishing times. The responsibility for, and the income from, these tourist businesses often remain in the hands of the women.

Although work in the tourist trade is in addition to their normal household duties, women on Caye Caulker claim they do not work much harder than before. This is due primarily to the increase in conveniences such as piped water, washing machines, and butane stoves. Ofilia Hernandez, who supported herself for years because of an early widowhood commented:

> Before I began the restaurant, I made coconut oil for B.25 cents a bottle. It was really hard work making coconut oil and bread with a coconut husk fire. And I earned less. Now I work the same but win more.

Jessica Barones, who is from one of the largest island families, is an example of an island woman whose life has been changed by tourism. She is married to Rogero, and they have a two year old son, Toby. Like many other women on Caye Caulker, she has put her culinary skills to work to make money. However, unlike most island women, Jessica has made her business a full-time occupation. She runs a pastry shop next to the Barones family house where she, her husband, and child are currently living. The shop belonged to her sister-in-law, Dalia, a Honduran who married into the Barones family. When Dalia and her husband, Elito Barones, moved to New York a few years ago, Jessica began to run the shop. "Jessica's Pastries," as she renamed the shop, is a popular place on the island. "Islanders buy from me more than they did from Dalia, because she's not from here," Jessica asserts.

As an islander, Jessica has also been able to acquire a piece of land at the new site near the cut. By writing a letter to the village council, she made herself eligible for the government raffle and became the first woman to participate. She and her husband have built a house 1/4 mile away, but have not moved in yet because she feels it is too far from the pastry shop.

Jessica spends most of her day in the shop, baking and selling to customers. Unlike other women, she is a breadwinner in her family, and she and her husband actively support one another's jobs. Every night he comes into the shop to squeeze 60 to 70 oranges for the bottles of juice she sells each day. In turn, Jessica has learned to stand up in front of Rogero's boat to find the lobster traps for him to haul up. "He helps me and I help him." she says.

This arrangement would be impossible without the help of Jessica's mother and sisters who take care of Toby and the shop on occasion and fix meals for the whole family. Family support makes it possible for Jessica to work. Jessica herself is often keeping an eye on Toby while she bakes, or she may close the shop to spend time with him if he is crying. Although she is economically self-sufficient, her summation of women's lives is very similar to that of other women: "They like to keep their home, always cleaning up, keeping the baby happy. They always think about that."

Jessica Barones is an enterprising young woman who has developed her own business with the help of a network of kin -- her father who built the pastry shop, her mother and sisters who help with child care, and her husband who participates in many ways in her work. Older women in more traditional situations also have been able to develop and expand their homes into a profitable tourist businesses. Sally Martin is an example of one of these women. Joe and Sally Martin have built a 12 room hotel on their land adjacent to their house. The Martins started with a club and theatre where they showed movies on the weekends, but they became dissatisfied with the club because of the noise, the drinking, and the late nights. Often, they would be awakened at 2:00 in the morning when someone wanted to buy a bottle of rum. The late nights were also hard on Joe who had to get up early in the morning to go fishing. The change to a hotel has eliminated these problems and has meant that much of the work of running the hotel has become Sally's. The jobs that Sally performs are all extensions of her traditional role as housekeeper and cook. Table II is a list of her daily jobs. When the hotel is full, the work keeps her busy all day. Her 19-year-old daughter is staying at home temporarily to help her mother with the hotel work. Although having the hotel work means she is occupied all day with cleaning and washing, Sally likes talking to the tourists, particularly those who come back year after year and stay for long periods of time.

During her free time she sews and talks with her daughter or her husband if it is too rough or rainy for him to go out fishing. She believes firmly in education, and all of her children have attended the secondary school in Belize City. Her two older children live in the United States, one daughter is a teacher in Belize City, and her son, recently married, lives on the island and visits daily, taking his meals with his mother. The youngest is currently studying in Belize City and lives with her older sister. Sally feels it is important for her daughters to

Table II. Daily Tasks in Hotel Work for Sally Martin

Housework	Make breakfast
	Wash the breakfast dishes
	Sweep and wash the floor
	Begin doing the day's load of laundry; hang to dry
	Mend and sew clothes
	Make lunch
	Wash the lunch dishes
	Sweep and clean the floor again
	Clean the bathroom - toilet, sink, and shower
	Prepare dinner for family
	Clean away dishes from dinner

Hotel Work	Cleaning rooms	Sweep floors
		Change sheets
		Dust mirrors

	Cleaning bathroom	Sweep floor
		Scrub sink and wash the mirror
		Scrub showers
		Clean toilets
		Put in new toilet paper

Sweep porch and outside floors

	Cooking for guests	Breakfast
		Dinner

Yard Work	Pot new plants
	Water the plants
	Rake the garden for leaves and weeds

---

get an education so they will be able to do something in
addition to having a home and marriage.

In the past, economic circumstances have meant that
women were completely dependent financially on a man.
Their lives have focused on the domestic sphere, not so
much because they had to be protected sexually but because
there was virtually no income-producing work for them.
The work women now do in the tourist trade is an extension
of their traditional duties and does not change their
domestic role. However, a woman can now bring in a
substantial income with tourist work, which represents a
significant change. It opens up the possibility for
women-headed households as a viable alternative to the
conjugal unit. It also reflects on the role of the man as
exclusive breadwinner.

Children

The socialization of children is primarily the
woman's responsibility. In the home, mothers teach
children their responsibilities and supervise their
behavior. In school, children are taught values along
with reading, writing, and arithmetic by the all-woman
staff. Children recognize three major influences on their
lives: being an islander, family, and school.

Being an islander involves a sense of ethnic history
that is kept alive primarily through language. Most
islanders are trilingual, and the children learn to speak
English, Creole, and Spanish interchangeably. More
important than their ethnic identity is the pride they
express in being from Caye Caulker. Children, from an
early age, learn to feel strong bonds to 'their' island.
As an islander, they learn to value independence, self-
sufficiency, responsibility, and tolerance of others. All
of these values are learned at home, at school, and in the
peer group games children play together.

Socialization in the Home

In the home children learn to respect adults by
speaking politely to them and helping them when asked.
Children are expected to help in the house and pick up
after themselves, although specific responsibilities
differ according to age and sex.

Children are also an important link between
households. They carry messages, run errands, and shop
for their mothers at the local stores. Children move

around the island more freely than do the adults and are an important link in the communication of information and gossip. The speed with which news travels from one end of the island to the other is partly explained by the role of children, who are very light-footed, in carrying this news.

Children are an important element in the distribution of food, both the information and the product itself. When a woman decides to offer a food for sale, she sends the children out to spread the word throughout the village. The children tell other villagers in the neighborhood and other children who then relay the information to their mothers. The women then pass the information along to their neighbors and friends, once again often using their children as messengers. The children take orders and return them to the woman producing the product. The villagers will then pick up their orders or the children may deliver them. For example, one day Elena Rivero decided to produce tamales, for sale. She sent Ricardo, a young man who works for her, to buy plaintain leaves for the tamales and he told several children to relay this information to their mothers. Elma Moreno received the information from one of her children. JoAnn Hettle heard it from Elma Moreno. Shirley Williams learned about it from Mrs. Gonzalez who made the masa Elena Rivero bought to make the tamales. As the tamales were being prepared, Ricardo repeatedly entered the kitchen with orders. In the final tally, Elena Rivero had orders for 66 tamales, which were then either delivered by Ricardo or picked up by women or children. Another way of distributing these homemade products is to fill a tub with the product and send the children out into the village to sell it.

Like adults, children on Caye Caulker are responsible for their own actions. They learn early to take care of themselves and to become independent. For example, if a child is injured, his family views the injury as the child's fault, and he may be reprimanded for not being more careful. Little boys are given fish knives to use and are expected to learn to be careful with them. If they cut themselves, it indicates they have not been using the knives correctly. Even as toddlers, children must learn to avoid the dangers of island life: falling off a pier, touching a Portuguese man-o-war, or stepping on broken glass or a conch shell. Once a mother was cleaning fish by the shore. Several times she warned her crawling child not to touch a man-o-war, whose sting is extremely painful. The child's curiosity prevailed, and he was badly stung. The mother continued to clean fish, ignoring the welts and the screams of the child who, she explained, had now learned never to touch a man-o-war. Children frequently learn through direct experience.

Children are expected to stay out of trouble, and injuries are viewed as an indication the child has done something wrong. One girl broke her toe while playing. Although it was a serious injury, she did not cry nor did she tell her father about it because he would get mad at her. Another time a young boy got badly cut when he was playing in the bush behind the school. Because he was not supposed to be playing in the bush, the principal scolded him when she found out. Children are often reluctant to go to an adult when they get hurt because they are then scolded.

Children are often teased by their parents, siblings, and relatives. They are expected to take the teasing without necessarily being taken in by it. For example, Cindy and her infant cousin, were often in the care of 14- year-old sister, Ruth. Ruth teased them by hiding from them, prodding them, or threatening to abandon them. Ruth was delighted when they started to cry.

> Want to see them cry. I can make him cry. Ta-ta. Ta-ta. (starts to leave the room and her infant cousin's face prunes up and he finally dissolves into tears). I love it when he cry. I like his face."

While the young children almost always get a hug afterward, they are nevertheless immediately teased again. Teasing can take four forms: hiding from the child, threatening to leave the child, threat of physical harm, and insults about appearance. Hiding and leaving evoke the most response, while insults about appearance are ignored and threats of harm are laughed off.

Even very young children learn how to respond to teasing. When adults relate to children by teasing, children are espected to stand up for themselves and trust their own resources rather than the adults. Jessica's little boy, Toby, at one and a half years old was teased one day by an uncle who poked a clothespin at him laughing cheerfully the whole time. "Toby, hold out your finger. Give me your finger, Toby" (click, click with the clothespin). Toby, frowning, looked very suspicious and put his hands into a tight fist, close to his chest, indicating that he knew what would happen if he stuck out his finger. Everyone laughed heartily at Toby's gesture.

Teasing, which seems to promote a 'sense of humor' as well as emotional independence, is complemented by early responsibility for household chores. Each child is responsible for specific household chores. Younger children, whose mothers bake bread or other goods, sell door-to-door in the afternoons, while older children are kept busy around the house. Although there are traditional male and female jobs, as with adults, household chores for children are not rigidly designated by gender.

For example, Maria Nanez is 13 years old and in her last year of school on Caye Caulker. She is the second youngest in a family of seven children. In the morning she makes her bed and sometimes washes the dishes before rushing to school to play with her friends. After school, she does her homework before going out to play hopscotch for awhile, and later she runs down to a store to pick up something for dinner. She may stop to deliver a message to relatives, her godmother, or her sister's boyfriend. Maria takes credit for getting her sister and her sister's boyfriend together because they often told each other 'hello' through Maria. She helps prepare dinner, though she sometimes finds cooking difficult, and her older sisters must help her. After dinner she does the dishes, sweeps, and tidies up. Maria does not want to go to high school in Belize City, even if she passes the entrance exam. She plans to stay home on Caye Caulker, help her mother around the house, and find a boyfriend. Alberto, who is in Maria's class at school, has a daily schedule very similar to hers. The main differences between them are the games they play (he prefers tops and soccer) and the household responsibilities (he must rake the yard, clear away grass with a machete, get ice from the co-op, and empty the garbage).

Primary School

Modeled after the British system, Caye Caulker has a primary school where children enter Infant school at four or five years of age and complete Standard Six at twelve or later. At school, children learn to read, write, and do math. There are approximately 140 students in three rooms taught by five teachers.

Infant I and II are taught in the largest room, where the four and five year olds spend most of their time sitting on the cement floor. Two teachers hold Standard 1-4 classes in the center room and two teachers share the north room with Standard 5 and 6 classes. With two classes going at once, the students must concentrate carefully to avoid being distracted by the other class.

School is also an important part of the socialization process. Teachers feel that one of their responsibilities is to teach the children how to behave. From the age of four, the children are expected to exhibit proper conduct. The younger children are expected to pay attention and answer questions. They also have to get their lessons checked. The older children are expected to have their homework done. They must keep up with a rigorous academic schedule. For example, in one hour the S5 and S6 classes covered six different readers. The classes are taught in English, though the students study Spanish as well. They are expected to use proper English at school, with no swear words and no Creole. They cannot talk back and are expected to answer their teachers politely, saying,"Yes, Miss Elma." School is considered more strict than home, and there are several other rules children listed:

- take turns answering questions
- don't cheat (look at others' papers, copy, use cribnotes)
- be at school
- don't go into the bush
- say the prayer and National Anthem
- line up at the sound of the bell
- don't interrupt the teacher or other students
- sit still
- don't talk behind people's backs
- don't laugh if someone makes a mistake
- show respect to older children
- don't quarrel
- obey older students or teachers
- play with other children
- be friendly
- don't curse
- do homework
- say you're sorry if you hurt someone
- don't talk when the teacher is talking

When children break these rules of behavior in school, several things may happen. The first and least severe is a 'scold,' a verbal reprimand. Students are 'scolded' by the teacher in front of the class when they do not do their homework, do not pay attention, talk while the teacher is talking, or fight with one another. Next, the student's ear gets pulled if he is not quiet after being scolded. Finally, a student who continues to misbehave will be 'lashed'. A rope with knots tied in the end is kept for this purpose, and although the principal says she does not use it anymore, the children believe that she might use it.

Since the island school is Catholic, religion is also taught. The students pray whenever they enter the classroom. After lunch a psalm or religious verse is sung. Schooling instills self-discipline, as well as religious values and respect for others. Values learned at school and at home are reflected in some of the games children play.

Games

Children play in groups, unsupervised, and generally without fighting. Although both boys and girls play ball games together at school, they seldom play together outside of school. Girls play many of the same games that boys do, but usually they play separately. They also enjoy games such as hopscotch or jump rope, which may have very complicated steps, but which are generally not competitive. If someone makes a mistake at jump rope, they merely laugh. The boys are much more competitive in their games. The main team sport played by the older boys is soccer, which is the most popular on the island. Among younger boys the game of tops became extremely popular one year. A top is a cylindrical wooden ball with a metal point at the more narrowly tapered end. In the game of tops as it is played on Caye Caulker, individuals can compete as seriously or lightly as they wish, can produce their own equipment, and can enter the game or leave at any time. It is not a very complex game. Basically, players compete to break one another's tops by the force of the spin. To begin a game, a line is drawn and everyone who wishes to play spins his top from behind the line. The person who shoots his top the farthest shoots first. Ranking of turns is determined by how far a person's top goes. The player who shoots the shortest distance starts the game by placing his top down in the center, while the other players try to break it. The active players who hit the top get to stay active and continue to take turns shooting at the top. If an active player does not hit the top, then he has to put his top down and let the player who was inactive play. Breaking this rule causes fights between players. Lewis explained that if someone refuses to put his top down after he missed, then other players get angry. When a fight occurs, the game often loses a player or two. New players join in at any point, and players constantly come and go.

The girls also like to play tops, but do not feel confident about playing with the boys. Once Amalia stood in the circle with the boys, rolled up a top, but never shot it. "I play tops but never with boys. My top would always be down if I played with boys," she said. When girls play they just throw the tops to try and hit the center, do not really take formal turns, and laugh a lot over it. The girls' version of tops is noncompetitive.

Secondary School

After finishing Standard Six, students may go to high school in Belize City if they pass the entrance exam. It is expensive to send a child to high school (about U.S.$150 per month), and most families try to arrange for them to stay with relatives. Parents encourage their children to continue their education, even though sometimes it is a great financial burden. However, if children at 12 or 13 do not want to continue with school, parents generally accept their wishes.

For example, Lon Barones stopped attending school after completing Standard 3. He works three days a week with his father hauling lobster traps, cleaning the lobster, and taking them to the co-op. He also helps his mother who runs a restaurant in her home by serving the tables and cleaning up afterwards. Marcia Barones also quit school after Standard 3 and spends her days taking care of the 3 year old baby and running errands. Both children want to stay on the island and get married.

According to the school principal, more girls go on to high school than boys since the boys can begin fishing and make more money than they could in positions that require a high school education. After graduation from high school, both girls and boys can get the same kinds of jobs in Belize City as bank tellers or office workers. But they seldom return to the island after high school, apart from the few women who come back to teach in the primary school. Those who do not go to high school stay with their families, and gradually take on greater responsibilities and independence until they set up their own domestic group.

Conclusions

On Caye Caulker, domestic groups contain both men and women and eventually children. Each person has a set of clearly defined responsibilities and jobs appropriate to his or her gender and age. These roles are viewed as complementary, and each member of the household, including children, contributes to the whole. Complementary roles are also viewed, loosely, as the natural order of things; however, there are no strict boundaries that are shameful or embarrassing to cross. As with all behavior on Caye Caulker, there is a tolerance of cross-role behavior as well.

The influx of tourism in the last ten years has created new economic opportunities for women on Caye Caulker. Although work in the tourist business has not altered the traditional domestic role of women, it does change their dependence on men as exclusive breadwinners. The development of a tourist business also provides the household with a seasonal income in addition to income from fishing, and thus creates a more balanced income-producing unit.

VI

Social Networks and Groups

On Caye Caulker, individuals value personal independence and self-sufficiency, and they respect these qualities in others. In the broadest sense, they translate these ideals into an unusual tolerance of a wide range of behavior and a community policy of non-interference in the lives of other islanders, non-islanders and even outsiders. In their relations with each other, and with the outside world, islanders espouse and defend their personal autonomy. At the same time, islanders combine this strong individualism with loyalty to kin. Loyalty to kin or family means to tolerate the behaviour of relatives at all times and to give financial assistance and personal support to family members. In turn, the individual draws support from kin networks for his endeavor to achieve economic self-sufficiency and personal independence. Consequently there is a congruence between, on the one hand, the goals of self-sufficiency, independence, and non-interference and, on the other hand, the ideals of family loyalty and the economic and social importance of being part of a family support network.

Family Loyalty

On Caye Caulker, loyalty to kin is an ideal and also a widespread reality. Kin have an obligation to help one another, to return favors, and to deal honestly and fairly with each other. Relationships between kin are expected to be closer and more dependable than relationships between non-kin. For example, if one member of a family becomes involved in a dispute, is sick, or is in trouble, his relatives will go to his aid immediately. Relations between friends who are not kin may also be friendly and helpful, and they may do favors for one another and exchange goods and services, but there is no hard and fast obligation to do so. Non-kin relationships are more fragile and less durable than kin relationships.

Members of extended families on Caye Caulker reinforce these obligations by participating in a system of reciprocal exchanges that have profound social and economic consequences. Socially these exchanges reinforce the solidarity of kin and provide evidence of the primacy of kin ties. Goods, services and favors are extended to kin on the assumption that they will be reciprocated later. However, the obligation of kin to one another exists even if it is not reciprocal. Some family members fail to reciprocate; nevertheless the obligation stands. For example, Simon has a cousin who drinks heavily and has a reputation for stealing. Simon's cousin uses all his money for rum and frequently relies on credit in Simon's store where he will run up a large bill. One day he came in and asked for a chicken so that 'my mother and brothers will have something to eat.' Simon refused and accused his cousin of stealing from his lobster traps. But finally Simon gave him a chicken and laughingly explained:

> I know they won't have anything to eat unless
> I give them this chicken. He promised to come
> pay me Friday, and I know that he will pay me
> with money he got selling the lobsters he
> stole from my traps on Thursday. They're
> never gonna pay me, but they're still family,
> see.

As is clear from this example, families support one another even if some members do not approve of the behavior of other. One large family, for instance, supports a family member who is a 'village drunk.' He spends his days drinking rum from the family-owned liquor store, his nights in rowdy, loud yelling and the early mornings retching and fighting off d.t.s. He does odd jobs around the kin locality and sometimes sells breadfruit from one of the trees for some rum money. His mother feeds him regularly, although he has in the past been so abusive to her at times that once the family arranged for her to leave the island for a year. Another time his arm was broken by a family member when his

behavior to one of the girls in the family became
intolerable.

Exchanges of Goods and Services

Family members interact daily. Most of this
interaction is based on a reciprocal exchange of goods and
services. These exchanges provide important economic
assistance to each household as well as functioning to
reinforce ideals of family loyalty.

Both women and men exchange raw and cooked food
regularly. When men arrive from fishing and clean their
lobster and fish on the pier at the kin locality,
relatives may walk down and ask for some of the catch.
Alternatively men may simply put aside certain portions of
the catch for particular family members and ask a child to
deliver it. Non-relatives may also be given a gift of
fish or they, and passing tourists, may purchase fish on
the pier. Raw fruits such as breadfruit, limes, and
coconuts are also given as gifts, and cooked foods such as
baked goods, coconut oil, bread, tamales, or a meal may be
given to a relative. These daily exchanges of food have
an important distribution function. Food items are not
always easily available, and since all food but fish,
coconuts and limes must be transported to the island,
these exchanges provide insurance against food shortages.
Being part of the food exchange network also reduces the
need for cash. One woman commented,

> I have just backed (carried) ten coconuts in a
> gunny sack to Anita (her husband's nephew's
> wife), for which I get one pint of coconut
> oil. Then I stopped by to pass the time of
> day with my mother-in-law and she gave me a
> sack of limes and a breadfruit.

It is also very common for relatives to eat with one
another regularly. Children from the kin locality in
particular are fed whenever they are present during a
meal. Adult children and relatives who do not, for
whatever reason, have a hot meal prepared for the day also
regularly eat with parents or relatives. Sally Martin's
uncle, who fishes with her husband Joe, takes his meals in
the Martin household. The two Moreno sons live apart from
their parents, but eat their meals at their parents'
house. In return they bring fish and lobster for their
parents to serve in their restuarant.

Although food is the most frequent item of exchange on Caye Caulker, child care is an equally important service, especially to the women. Children go freely to the homes of relatives and eat there. When a mother has work to do, a female relative will take care of a small child. Sometimes an older sibling will be responsible for a young child, but on Caye Caulker, infants and toddlers are generally under the responsibility of an adult relative rather than young siblings. Jessica Barones' sister watches her son Toby or helps in the bakery when Jessica herself has to attend to Toby, and she is given baked goods in return. School age children who must live in Belize City to study are housed with a relative. Ruby and Alberto Sanchez stay with their mother's sister in Belize City and Peter Williams, Jr. sends his children to his mother's house there. All of these arrangements are reciprocated with other goods and services in preference to payment in cash. For example, families from Caye Caulker stay with relatives when they visit Belize City and families from Belize come to Caye Caulker for vacations such as Easter. In one case, a man was left with ten children to raise when his wife abandoned him, and his sister raised them. She is unmarried and makes a living selling bread, coconut oil and soft drinks from her house. The children lived with their father but stopped by her house daily to be fed.

Finally, family members also share transportation into Belize City and back. Ned Williams often rode with his brother Simon who, because he was running a store on the island, had to make frequent trips to stock his shelves. Joe Martin, Jr. gives his family transportation when they need it and in return, his parents recruit hotel guests to ride with him as paying passengers. While in Belize City family members pick up mail or run errands for one another. Relatives also help each other with tasks that require special skills. When Ned Williams was building a boat his father's wife sewed the sails for him. When Ned's uncle died, Ned built the coffin.

Occasional Work Groups

Men who are relatives also cooperate on projects that require a group of men. Sometimes, friends and others who are not particularly busy at the time, or who enjoy the company and a shared bottle of rum, will join these work groups, but they have no obligation to do so. For instance, boats have to be hauled up on the beach

every three months to be scraped and painted. A sail boat
and even a skiff will require several men to haul up.
When a group assembles for this task, it also becomes a
social event. Ned's wife described one such occasion:

> Yesterday we woke up at 4:30 a.m. to haul up
> the boat. Ned carried all the belongings from
> the boat, the sails, floorboards, and ballast.
> Frank, my brother-in-law, said we could haul
> up by his house which is only ten feet from
> the water, and close enough to get electricity
> to sand the boat. Ned dragged the boat in the
> water two blocks down to Frank's, like a small
> tug towing the Queen Elizabeth. He told me to
> go to Luciano's bar and get a quart of
> Caribbean rum and three cokes. "Who wants rum
> at seven in the morning," I asked. "It's the
> custom" he replied. At Frank's house there
> were about twelve men pulling up the boat with
> a long rope. There was a lot of laughter and
> much talk, with everyone telling everyone else
> how to put the rollers (coconut trunks) under
> the boat so it rolls up onto the beach. When
> they finished, they fell to on the quart of
> Caribbean Rum.

Work groups also form when a catastrophe strikes or
there is some natural disaster. One day there was a huge
storm, and it knocked over one of the outhouses at the end
of a pier. For a while everyone in the Williams kin
locality had to use Ted Williams's outhouse. For one old
lady it was a precarious negotiation to get to the
outhouse further away, even when helped by her
grandchildren. Five men organized a work group, lifted
the outhouse back onto the pier, and reinforced it with
planks. Then a bottle of rum was shared among the men.

Work Partnerships

Relatives also cooperate in a variety of ways in
their work. A young man learns to fish with a father or
uncle. Later he may become partners with a relative and
share in the work and profits from fishing together.
Relatives will loan fishing equipment such as skiffs, nets
and tools. A father may give his son his first boat and
motor. Eventually a man will inherit a lobster territory

from a relative or begin one adjacent to that of a
relative.

Some families on Caye Caulker have become partners
in business. The Lenos family is a good example of how a
family partnership works. Ramon Lenos owns a hotel and
restaurant. He and his brother Eduardo started out as
fishing partners, but when the tourist business began to
take more and more of their time, Ramon asked Eduardo to
help him out. Eduardo commented,

> I didn't think twice about working for Ramon
> even though I don't have to. But I see that
> it's all in the family and I know if in the
> course of a year I need some cash, he would
> give it to me.

Eduardo was laid up for years by a very serious boating
accident. During this time, Ramon supported Eduardo and
his family and continues to do so because Eduardo is not
completely back on his feet. When the business began to
boom, Ramon's sons, who are in high school in Belize,
could not help their father. Ramon asked Rafael,
Eduardo's son, to work in the ice cream palour. Rafael
began by working for a couple of days but was needed more
and more often and finally began to work full time.
Rafael worked much longer hours than he would normally
because he was willing to be part of a family business.
Eduardo's wife often helps out by cleaning the hotel and
Ramon's wife and daughters also help as cooks. One of the
reasons that tipping is not customary in businesses on
Caye Caulker is that most of the work is done, not by wage
earners, but by family members who share in the profits.

There is some indication that reciprocity based on
exchanges of goods and services may be moving to a more
cash-based set of economic transactions. In the last few
years, transportation to Belize has become less easy to
obtain on a casual exchange basis. Because gasoline for
the motors on skiffs is now so expensive, and anyone
making a trip to Belize can charge tourists for a place,
islanders have begun charging each other as well. Close
family members still provide transportation as a service,
but non-family, and sometimes distant relatives, are now
having to pay on a regular basis. Hotel and restaurant
work also may be turning to wage labor. As the tourist
trade develops, businesses on Caye Caulker need more labor
and are developing a wage earning force. Wage labor is
already more prevalent on San Pedro although there are

still family run businesses there as well. As yet, there are very few wage laborers on Caye Caulker and most of them are non-islanders.

Interaction with Non-Family

Regardless of family affiliation, or place of origin, islanders believe that individuals, not the family or community, are responsible for their own actions. Even a child is expected to be responsible for his own safety. Along with this emphasis on personal responsibility, islanders also uphold the right of individuals to determine their own actions. Accordingly no one has a right to dictate anyone else's behavior, even if that behavior impinges on the well-being of others. A man who drinks heavily or goes on drinking binges will be tolerated or even aided. Other islanders will loan him money, buy him drinks, feed him, or listen to him patiently during a drunken monologue. When he passes out, someone will pull him into the shade. Though many people disapprove of drunkenness, they rarely express their disapproval publicly or to the drunken person himself, even when he might be abusive or threatening. Occasionally if he really goes too far or becomes too threatening, someone might take action. But the situation soon returns to normal, and the behavior is ignored.

The island view that each person is responsible for his own actions and should not interfere with others is illustrated by the reaction to theft. One of the villagers has a reputation for stealing women's underwear off clotheslines in the dead of night, usually after a drinking bout. The islanders protect themselves from his thievery simply by never leaving their underwear on the line past sundown. One woman woke during the middle of the night, suddenly remembering that her clothes were still out on the clothesline. Too tired to go out and bring them in, she went back to sleep. The next morning they were gone. She blamed only herself, not the thief, since she knew she should not have left them on the line.

Individualism and personal responsibility for one's own actions in conjunction with tolerance and non-interference with regard to the actions of others are the basis for interaction with non-family, both islanders and non-islanders. Most community organizations on Caye Caulker are very weak. The cultural rules for social interactions, which are well suited to relations between individuals, make formal organization extremely difficult.

How will the organization be run, and by whom? Islanders
are reluctant to interfere in their neighbor's lives, and
they also staunchly oppose any efforts by their neighbors
to assert authority over them. They resent the external
authority of the Belizean government in the form of laws,
institutions, and health and law enforcement personnel.
However, they do not look much more favorably upon locally
organized government. Neither level of government has
much legitimate authority on Caye Caulker, and both are
forced to rely on consensus and voluntary compliance.

<u>Daily Interaction</u>

Socializing or 'flapping around' is a favorite
activity of people on Caye Caulker. Socializing breaks up
the routine of daily chores and is an important part of
some tasks. Women spend most of their day in the home and
are more isolated than men, though they may visit
relatives briefly during the day just to chat or to pass
on some information.   Men tend to do more casual
socializing. They often congregate in small groupson the
piers while they clean lobster or fish.   They may spend
time at the co-op receiving station, joking with their
neighbors as they bring in their catches.   Some heavy
jobs, such as hauling up boats for maintenance, require a
crew of several men, who are recruited among family and
non-family.   These jobs sometimes become social events
when, after the work is done, the men relax under a
coconut tree and share a bottle of rum and some
conversation.
In the evenings, when work is finished, men tend to
congregate in neutral places outside of family localities.
Some men go to bars to drink and talk with other islanders
or tourists. However, more often they just gather on the
corners of lanes and talk for hours. In this way island
news is passed on during the course of the evening. Most
groups do not gather on family-owned land. "The neutral
gathering place is right there where the roads meet...Most
people call it 'the lane'. They say, 'I'm going to the
lane.'"
Before the tourist trade picked up, whole families
used to go down to the piers in the evening to enjoy the
cool breeze from the sea and visit with their neighbors
and relatives. But nowadays women are most apt to stay at
home unless they attend evening church services at the
Assemblies of God church. During the tourist season they

may have extra work to finish in the evening, and many enjoy just relaxing and watching television.

Aside from the pure pleasure of one another's company, socializing provides the means for keeping up with what is happening on the island. In a community as small as Caye Caulker, where eveyone knows everyone else, there is inevitably a lot of gossip. Most of the islanders are keenly interested in their neighbors' lives. When Ned Williams left Caye Caulker for a visit to the States, he was bored the whole time he was away from the island. Not the least interested in all the new attractions of the U.S., he worried about what he was missing on Caye Caulker.

News travels quickly from one end of the island to the other, and commonly within an hour of an incident, everyone has heard about it in all its detail. However, in spite of the speed with which gossip travels, a 'mind your own business' attitude prevails. Islanders are taught from childhood not to interfere in other people's lives, with the assumption that others will not interefere with theirs. Although in such a small place people eventually know everything that happens, that knowledge does not lead to any kind of action. Further, the islanders' extreme tolerance is translated into little public censure of other people's actions.

It would be wrong to give the impression that people on Caye Caulker never disagree with each other or fall out. Sometimes there are disputes between whole families, but usually disagreements occur between individuals. Fights about stealing and sexual infidelity are the most common, though little or no action is taken over these issues. Furthermore, certain people are considered 'no good' and are avoided because of their past actions. For example, when a known troublemaker returned to Caye Caulker after two and a half years in prison, the whole island was suspicious of him.

> He is continually watched by everyone here. No one ever turns his back to him. No one talk to him. Everyone is convinced that it is only a matter of time until he does something else to be sent back to prison.

Generally, those who steal or break the accepted rules in other ways are well-known to other islanders, who keep a constant watch on them.

The Caye Caulker way of dealing with unpleasant and potentially devisive situations is avoidance rather than confrontation. Islanders simply ignore the person and resolutely carry on with their own lives. People who have seriously offended one another - by adultery or theft- live next door to each other and to all appearances calmly lead their own lives.

Island-Wide Organizations

We have already seen that support networks among family members function very effectively partly because they are based on loyalty and trust. The success or failure of island-wide organizations, however, depends primarily on the particular needs they meet and how they are initiated and structured. Organizations which are locally initiated are far more successful than those imposed from the outside. Moreover, organizations based on equality among members gain more rapid acceptance than those based on authority.

The Co-op

The co-op is clearly the most successful organization on Caye Caulker. Its success can be attributed to several factors. First, although it is a national organization it was locally organized by the fishermen themselves, and they still have control of the Managing Committee. This is consistent with the island ideal of local control and autonomy from outside. Secondly, it is essentially an association of equals with each member having an equal vote and a share of the profits based on individual production levels. The Managing Committee, elected by the members, has considerable power within the co-op organization; however, they are accountable to the members at large and if they abuse their power they will not be returned to office. Third, the co-op is well managed and efficient, partly because the islanders actively participate in its operation and partly because the Managing Committee has been an effective group. Last, but perhaps most important, the co-op has made huge profits, and each member has been able to improve significantly his own economic position.

In comparing the Caye Caulker cooperative with other fishermen's cooperatives, it is clear that it has all the ingredients of success. In a review of the literature on

the formation of cooperatives in fishing communities,
James Acheson maintains that they are organized "when
fishermen have been or feel badly used by buyers, and join
together to get fairer prices and steadier markets for
their fish . . . In short, cooperatives are often formed
as a strategy to regain control over capital equipment and
maintain independence, not just to gain competitive prices
for fish."[1] Although it is difficult to generalize about
the success or failure of cooperatives, Acheson has
determined that, "cooperatives tend to succeed when
fishermen gain benefits in terms of better prices,
favorable loans, services at reasonable fees, more stable
supplies of fish and stabler prices, and *where the
cooperative is organized in a way that the fishermen feel
it is theirs*." (italics mine)[2]. The important factor
seems to be that in successful cooperatives, the
organization is compatible with the culture as a whole and
does not impinge on the independence of individuals within
the fishing community.

How does the success of the Northern Fishermen's
Cooperative compare with other cooperatives in Belize that
have been less successful? The main fishing cooperatives
other than the Northern are the National Co-op in Belize
City, the Caribeña in San Pedro and cooperatives in
Placentia and Sartenejo. Both Placentia and Sartenejo
have had problems due to their distance from Belize City
where produce must be delivered. For Sartenejo fishermen,
for example, it soon became apparent that both the
collection of ice and delivery of produce would be more
convenient as well as economical if they used the Northern
facilities either in Caye Caulker or in Belize City rather
than return to Sartenejo each trip. When large numbers of
fishermen joined the Northern, the Sartenejo Co-op folded.
Apart from the disadvantage of distance, all four
cooperatives have had another kind of problem. Precisely
because of the success of the Northern Fishermen's
cooperative in securing advantageous bids on produce and
therefore paying larger dividends, members of other
cooperatives find it more profitable to join the Northern.
Success draws members from other cooperatives and at the
same time spells their end by shrinking them to a no
longer viable size.

James Gregory has reported that in Belize there have
been many failed cooperatives causing one Belizean
government official to remark "Co-ops are a joke; they
don't work."[3] However, he argues very effectively that
even cooperatives that eventually fail as an economic

enterprise, often act as vehicles for social change. The Mayan Cooperative and later the Mopan Cooperative of San Antonio, he maintains, did much to develop the economic and political aspirations of younger members of the community and had an important positive impact on education, economic development and political participation.[4]

Churches

Religion arrived on Caye Caulker with the first Mestizo settlers who brought their Catholic faith with them from Yucatan. The first church was built in the 1880's. It was used occasionally when priests from Belize City came out to the island to perform services, but there were no regular weekly services. Everyone on the island was at least nominally Catholic, but without a priest or much organization, religious beliefs persisted primarily on a personal level. Only within the last two decades have priests begun coming out to the island from Belize City on a regular weekly basis to conduct Sunday workshop services. In 1982 a cement block church was constructed, and in 1983-84 six lay ministers were ordained from among the islanders, after ten months of study. These lay ministers are now qualified to lead worship services. Each oversees a specific part of church activities, such as Sunday School or building maintenance. However, church members do not recognize in them the same religious authority and knowledge the priest has, and services conducted by the priest are much better attended than those led by the lay ministers.

The Catholic Church had been the only religious body on the island for nearly a century when protestant missionaries began arriving one by one about twenty years ago. Initially they had little impact; however, about five years ago, Vito was 'saved', and the Assemblies of God church gained a foothold on Caye Caulker. According to his sister, Vito had been leading a "life of sin" in Belize City, when he was witnessed to by a man from the Assemblies of God church.

> He got saved. He accepted the truth of the gospel and accepted Jesus Christ as his personal saviour. He made a bargain in his heart to start a church on the island where he had been born. He wanted to help the people of Caye Caulker.

Soon a pair of missionaries began making trips out to Caye Caulker from Belize City to witness and preach. The Assemblies of God church slowly gained members on the island. In the first year it took in ten members. Recently that increased to eighteen, in comparison to the more than 350 members of the Catholic Church. The church drew mainly from Vito's relatives - his mother, his sister and her husband, several members of the Martin kin group, and a few women who are unrelated to either of the groups.

In 1982, they constructed a cement block church and hired their first minister, a Guatemalan. The church is extremely active, with services Sunday morning and almost every week night. The members participate enthusiastically in the services, and the minister also encourages them to take time to visit their neighbors and witness to them. However, this conflicts so strongly with the Caye Caulker rule of non-interference that he has thus far been unsuccessful in this endeavor.

Although it is small, the Assemblies of God church has brought some significant changes on the island. Because it believes in active conversion rather than non-interference and because by church standards virtually all non-converted islanders are sinners, there is a clash of values between the converted and unconverted. For example, the church takes a strong stand against drinking and adultery. According to several men and their wives, their conversion has improved their family lives because the men spend more time at home and do not drink. However, it has also divided families. For example, if only one spouse converts, inevitably a tension between husband and wife results. In several cases conversion has also strained or caused severed relations between kin and between friends. In some cases, this has resulted in a break in the traditional kinship support networks. Many Catholics feel somewhat threatened or betrayed by the converts, while members of the Assemblies of God church feel some anger towards the Catholic church, as they believe that a 'personal relationship with Jesus Christ' is not possible within the Catholic doctrine. Further, they strongly disapprove of many of the actions of some members of the Catholic church, for instance, drinking or carrying on visiting relationships. Some Assemblies of God members have severed relations with friends or relatives whose actions they believe are immoral. The Assemblies of God church is the only force that has been able to erode wider family support networks on Caye

Caulker, an indication of the depth of its current strength. A woman whose family converted after her daughter was healed at a prayer session aptly described the dilemma of conversion:

> We all got saved . . . It was like a bomb dropped on the Catholic church. They even called a priest from the United States to convince us to come back. Our best friends turned their backs on us. I remember on my birthday, standing looking out my window with tears streaming down my face because all my friends left me. But I had found a new friend - Jesus.

Service Organizations

Other locally organized groups have been much less successful. Though they may be locally organized, the islanders generally see little need for such groups. For example, the Caye Caulker chapter of the Lion's Club, a service organization which contributed the swings for the local park, appears and disappears quickly. Concern that one person may be benefiting more than others from the group's activities leads to its dissolution, until someone decides to try to reorganize and revitalize it.

There is also a Youth Group on the island, which is fairly inactive. Raphael Lenos explained, "We used to clean the beaches, all around the island. By the time we finished, we'd have to start over again. But we can't co-operate any more to get it done, so we don't do it anymore." The group's activities are currently limited to planning occasional dances or parties.

A couple of islanders have made several attempts to start a hotel or tourist association to set uniform prices in the tourist industry. But local business owners "couldn't co-operate. Because they have their own money now, they don't need others."

Part of the failure of these groups can be attributed to the low priority islanders assign to service to the community in comparison with loyalty to family. Moreover islanders see little need for cleaned beaches or business associations. In some cases islanders are also suspicious that some individuals may use the organization to better their own positions at the expense of others or to gain some measure of authority over others.

Village Council

Forms of government imposed by the national
government are not particularly effective either, unless
they have a specific task at hand which islanders support.
For instance, the Village Council generally has little to
do and does not have a great deal of authority, though it
may be activated by natural disasters or other problems
which occur sporadically. Its responsibilities include
keeping public property (the community center, cemetery,
police station, and park) in good repair, representing the
Belizean government on Caye Caulker, and collecting land
taxes, which remain on Caye Caulker as operating funds for
the Village Council. Other taxes and license fees are paid
directly to the government in Belize City. Most people
have few dealings with the Village Council, and when
problems do arise they are more likely to view Louis
Sylvestre, their elected representative to the Belizean
National Assembly as the more legitimate liaison with the
national government.

Elections for the Village Council are held every two
years, and people can serve as many terms as they continue
to be elected. By their own choice, they are not paid,
although the government thinks they should receive a
percentage of tax money collected. Actually, there is
usually so little interest in the Village Council that
Eduardo Lenos once served for several years without being
re-elected, because no one else wanted to be on it. No
one ran or came to the meetings. Louis Sylvestre
organizes the election meeting. After seven to ten people
are nominated, a vote is taken and the top seven vote-
getters are elected. They decide among themselves who
will hold the various positions, ranging from chairman to
'wise owl', who reports any illegal businesses or other
problems to the board. For example, if tourists are
charging people to go to the reef or setting up a business
on the island, then the 'wise owl' brings this to the
attention of the Village Council.

The Village Council is required to hold a general
meeting every year to report their activities and
expenditures to the public, though they are not
necessarily prompt in doing this. They may have one or
two other public meetings during the year if specific
problems come up, for instance, if taxes are not up-to-
date or some kind of disaster strikes. However, most of

the Village Council meetings are closed, and the
secretary's notes are not available for islanders to read.

Land Committee

The five-year Land Committee is an extension of the
Village Council. Its objective is more concrete. It was
created for the purpose of parcelling out the land at the
Cut. It is responsible for screening and selecting
applicants and distributing the land through a lottery
system. Once this task has been completed, the committee
will probably be dissolved.

Justice of the Peace

The office of Justice of the Peace is an unpaid
legal office. The individual JP is appointed by the
Belizean government and is always an islander. A Justice
of the Peace is responsible for seeing that 'law and order
are kept on the island', signing legal papers, and
performing marriage ceremonies. There are two Justices of
the Peace on Caye Caulker, Eduardo Lenos and Luciano
Martin. Eduardo has been a Justice of the Peace since
1974, when he received an unexpected letter informing him
that he would be appointed Justice of the Peace if he
would accept the position. He once tried to resign the
post, but the government strongly discouraged him from
doing so.
Neither the Village Council nor the Justices have a
great deal of authority. Islanders prefer to abide by
their unwritten code of non-interference with individuals'
rights rather than formalized laws and methods of
enforcement. Thus, organizations or offices imposed by
the national government must rely largely on voluntary
compliance, and when this fails the case is most often
simply handed over to the Belizean government, which
handles fines and punishments.

School

The one exception to the generally weak government-
imposed organizations is the school. The school is
supported by islanders for two reasons. First, it is
staffed by islanders. The principal is both an islander
and a teacher. Second, the islanders generally value an
education. They recognize that Caye Caulker has never
been able to support a large population and that there

will always be some young who want to leave. Therefore, islanders want their children to get a basic education so that they can be prepared for further schooling in Belize City and eventually for jobs elsewhere. Girls especially have been encouraged to continue with schooling because they had no other means of attaining economic independence. It is generally agreed that those who stay on the island also require an education. First, there is more and more need to deal with the outside, both through fishing and tourist business. Second, fishermen who expect to run their own cooperative successfully must be educated as well. The co-op, for example, has financed the higher education of several men in training programs abroad.

Government Officials

Nonislanders who are sent by the Belizean government to fill official positions of policeman and nurse on Caye Caulker represent the least effective form of authority. As outsiders in roles imposed from the outside, they have little basis of legitimacy in the islander's view and violate the local ideal of noninterference.

A government nurse is regularly assigned to Caye Caulker although frequently there is no nurse residing on the island at any one time. She lives in the community center where she has a clinic from which she dispenses medication and administers first aid and immunizations to babies and children. Though many islanders believe it is a good idea to have a nurse, they are accustomed to self-reliance and self-medication, sometimes with herbal remedies; therefore, many do not use her services. Most islanders prefer to go directly to Belize City for emergencies or to the United States or Mexico for serious illnesses and surgery. Expectant mothers also go to Belize City for delivery, although for many years an elderly islander was the local midwife. The nurse's role is primarily as a public health officer. In this role, she is often perceived as an 'interference', by the islanders.

For example, in January 1983, a handful of malaria cases appeared on the island. In an attempt to kill off the malaria-carrying mosquitoes, the nurse requested the government send out a crew to spray inside all houses and hotels with a mixture of kerosene and DDT. The reaction of the islanders was hostile. Some questioned whether or not the cases were really malaria. Many refused to allow their houses or hotels to be sprayed. One hotel owner who refused to allow spraying in either her house or hotel, described her encounter with the 'spraymen'.

> I told them, 'I have a clean house, and there are no bugs in it.' I told them I had a sick baby in the house and I was sick too, so they couldn't spray. That wasn't true. They threatened to take me to court. But I said, 'I'm not a thief.I don't kill. So I'm not afraid of any court.' They went away then, but they had the police call me and tell me they would take me to court. But I told them the same thing.

The government assigns two policemen to Caye Caulker and tries to achieve an ethnic balance by sending one Creole and one Spanish policeman. The most serious local crimes include stealing lobster skiffs and their motors, and personal property from houses left unattended. There is a small amount of vandalism as well. Some crimes are directed against tourists, but islanders also have to be very careful to avoid being robbed. Houses are locked and watched by relatives when people are away, and even then thieves are sometimes successful. One Martin family was robbed of several thousand dollars of jewelry while visiting relatives in Belize City. One man reportedly had six motors stolen from him in one year. Although in several cases, he knew who took them, he took no action against the thief. Valuable property such as motors and gas tanks are now brought in from skiffs every evening and secured next to the house.

There is some indication that personal assault, usually by groups of young men, referred to as 'no good' by islanders, is on the rise. In one case a long term foreign resident was so badly beaten by a group of young men, alledgedly for complaining to the police about the shooting of endangered species of birds, he left the island permanently. Trouble may also flare up between policemen and the young island men when the policemen try to enforce any kind of discipline. One young man recounted a small confrontation with the police.

> One night I was in front of Bob Rodrigues' with some guys. Bob called the police because he said we were making too much noise. The police came down and told us to leave, you

know. Try to show their power, man. They try
to rule here. No way man. We told them
'Forget it, man, we aren't going nowhere. We
rule here, man.'

In December, 1983, a local policeman was assaulted
by a group of 'boys' and badly beaten.

From the government point of view, serious crimes
include assault of policemen, drug dealing (by Belizeans
and foreigners) and contraband smuggling (consumer goods
from Chetumal and drugs). Although crimes of personal
violence have, until very recently, been rare on Caye
Caulker, these crimes will be difficult to control without
a central authority such as that represented by the
policeman.

Conclusions

The success of any social organization on Caye
Caulker depends on two key factors: the perceived need for
such an organization and whether it is initiated by
islanders or outsiders. This relation can be illustrated
diagramatically as follows:

Figure III: Relative Effectiveness of Organizations on
Caye Caulker

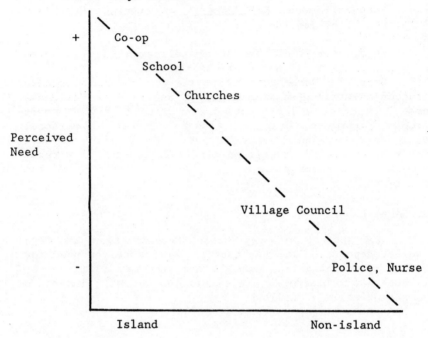

The dotted line in the graph represents the relative effectiveness of the organizations. The co-op, locally organized and locally run, is at the top. Institutions such as the school and the churches, though connected with large external organizations, are essentially locally run. Also, they provide a function that the islanders value. The Village Council, a form imposed from the outside to meet a need the islanders seldom see, is much less effective. Least effective are offices or organizations that violate the island rule of noninterference, are imposed from the outside, and held by nonislanders.

NOTES

1.   Acheson, James, <u>Anthropology of Fishing</u>, Ann. Rev. Anthropol, 1981, p. 284.

2.   <u>Ibid</u>, page 285.

3.   Gregory, James R., "Cooperative: 'Failures' Versus 'Successes',   <u>Belizean Studies</u>, Vol, 12, No. 5, 1984, page 1.

4.   <u>Ibid</u>, page 9, 12-15.

VII

Tourism

During the past 15 years, thanks primarily to the
Co-op, Caye Caulker has become an affluent community
relative to the rest of the country. More recently,
tourism has also grown. These new cash resources and the
influx of visitors have, in turn, brought considerable
change to the island and its people.

On my first trip to Caye Caulker in 1972, there were
no hotels and no restaurants. I slept on the beach and
had to ask another foreigner to give me food. At that
time, one could count on one hand the foreigners on Caye
Caulker: Annette, an American woman in her 50's was on
Caye Caulker to spend her last days dying of cancer;
Frank, an odd job man from Florida who married a young
Belizean woman and lived on Caye Caulker for several years
eking out a living through diving and charging the
occasional visitor for a trip to the reef. These
foreigners were oddities, frequently casualties of
"modern" society. One engineer, who had worked for years
at Cape Canaveral finally buckled under the stress of
countdowns and small screens. He suffered from bleeding
ulcers and endured a mental breakdown. When doctors in
Houston gave up trying to cure him, he came to Caye
Caulker, sat in a Mennonite rocking chair, ate papaya for
six months, and returned to the U.S. a new man. Caye
Caulker cures for American civilization were a common
feature of these early visitors. A no less colorful
figure was that of the modern day pirate. People arrived

regularly with a 'story' and a 'past' and usually some scheme for making a fortune. One year a man in a medical orderly shirt arrived on Caye Caulker. Almost never sober, breathing rum in my face, he announced to all that he was a free mason and an anthropologist, a psychologist and a professor of art and a stone mason as well (he was later dubbed the stoned free mason). Or there was the group referred to as 'the Texans', a crowd of time-warp 60's hippies who come every year to the 'Caribbean Inn' to whoop it up on beer and marijuana and re-experience the 60's. One of them is called 'Shark Bait' apparently because his friends once dragged him, in a drug-induced stupor, along the reef to attract sharks. Proud of his story he has had it immortalized on his arm in the form of a tatoo: a naked woman riding a shark. Underneath the legend reads: "Shark Bait."

Gradually more and more foreigners, young and generally adventuresome, began to discover Caye Caulker, learning about the island by word of mouth. A 29-year-old carpenter from Kansas, told the following story:

> It was just an accident that I first came to Caye Caulker when I was 21. I was hanging out in Merida waiting for a friend when I met Mike. I told him I was heading for Peru. He said, 'Hey, you're going that far south, are you going through Belize on your way south?' and I said 'Where?' He said 'Belize'. I said, 'Belize, I've never heard of it,' and he said, 'Well, it used to be British Honduras'. I had heard of British Honduras, but still I couldn't place it. 'Well it's the next country south. You won't miss anything by going through it. If you want to go to Guatemala you might as well see Belize.' He told me about Caye Caulker and all the fishing out here, and I love to dive and spear fish so I came out here for about three days when I met some National Geographic photographers who were headed for Tikal and asked me to come along. We were hanging out in the jungle for three days and I was lying in my hammock one night, and I decided to come back to Caye Caulker. I decided to come back for a week and ended up staying four months. I have come back every year since then.

Initially a haven mainly for backpackers working their way down the 'Central American trail', Caye Caulker now attracts a wide range of young (25-35 year old) American, Canadian, and European travellers of the more adventurous nature. Many of these adventurers use Caye Caulker as a pleasant island break before heading off for the more politically unstable areas of Guatemala, El Salvador, Honduras and Nicaragua. Others come for the diving on the reef after becoming disenchanted with resorts like Cancun or Cozumel. Or they sail down on their sailboats and anchor for awhile at Caye Caulker where they can purchase supplies and take advantage of the bars in the evening. For others Caye Caulker offers a regular escape from Northern winters or restricting jobs. Such visitors return again and again, settling on Caye Caulker for a few winter months of island sun, diving, drinking rum and smoking pot before returning to their job in April or May. All of these travellers are attracted to the unpretentious fishing village appearance of Caye Caulker and to the very lack of luxurious amenities. For their part, the islanders seem to like the younger, less conventional crowd of visitors and make little effort to attract the tourist market that demands hot water and air conditioning.

The proliferation of modern schemers and pirates on Caye Caulker and in other areas of Belize has recently received attention in the U.S. press. The Washington Post (January 27, 1985) carried an article entitled "Mildewed Intrigue at Land's End: All That Changes in Belize are the Fantastic Sun-Baked Schemes" (by Ken Ringle)

> In the smoldering Central America of the 1980s, however, Belize has come of strategic age. Tiny as it is, its position at the foot of Mexico makes it a potentially unyielding domino, across whose notoriously porous borders any major arms shipments from Cuba or Nicaragua would logically travel.

> "Living in Belize is like living in Casablanca," said ex-patriate American William Harmon one night over a Belikan beer in San Pedro. "About three times a day, somebody comes up to you with a fantastic scheme of some kind for making a fortune. It may involve smuggling or drugs or timbering or Mayan artifacts or just development

investment.   But the figure is always the
same: $2 million."

That endangered species, the soldier of
fortune, still thrives in Belize.

As visitors began to appear in larger and larger
numbers during the seventies the need for sleeping and
eating facilities became apparent.   Edith's hotel,
constructed by enclosing the area under the house into
small cubicles, was one of the first places on the island
to offer accommodation. Other places quickly followed
suit, and gradually people began to build separate
'hotels' on their land next to their homes. Women began
to prepare meals to serve in renovated rooms or to sell
cooked food out the window to tourists walking down the
sand lanes. Eventually extra 'dining rooms' were added on
to houses, and in the last few years restaurants separate
from dwellings now operate daily to serve the increasing
number of visitors. By the late 1970's, apart from a
slump in tourism in 1982 due to the devaluation of the
peso in Mexico, during the peak of the tourist season,
January, as many as 200 tourists would be on Caye Caulker
at one time, but the rest of the year, the number ranges
from 20 to 50. As one man put it, "January is a squall,
the rest of the year it drizzles."
     The tourist 'industry' on Caye Caulker has grown
slowly, as the islanders invested only limited capital and
time in it. However, by the 1980's tourism had become an
attractive means of making extra money during the winter
season. For example, Hershey has for many years provided
regular transportation by skiff from Caye Caulker to
Belize City. Proud of his ability to provide a service
that tourists need - reliable transportation - Hershey
makes a very good living (U.S.$35,000 per year
approximately) entirely from tourism and is developing
boat tours of inland sites and nearby islands. Only a few
islanders depend solely on tourism for an income, however,
and most do not fare quite as well as Hershey. Richard,
for example, earns $30,000 per year from lobster traps,
but in addition he runs a hotel and two rental houses and
repairs skiff motors. His wife teaches school and his two
sons also haul traps when they are on vacation from
school. Each son earns approximately $7,000 each per
year.
     In 1983, twelve hotels, ranging from four to a
couple dozen rooms per hotel, accommodated tourists coming

to the island. Eating places included a pastry shop or two, five small restaurants, and five individuals who served dinner to people with reservations. Caye Caulker has increasingly moved towards tourism as a source of income. Many young men and women are developing tourist businesses as a full-time occupation and some older men, who in their later years find fishing too physically taxing, are retiring to run hotels and other businesses. Thus, a dual economy balanced between fishing and tourism, is emerging on Caye Caulker. Furthermore, the pattern developed in the fishing business, of local control of resources by local islanders, seems to be repeating itself in the development of tourism.

However, investment in tourism has a number of disadvantages. It does not represent real development, and the number of tourists are subject to the fluxes of foreign economies. A recession in the United States or Europe has an instant impact on the number of tourists that come to the island. The recent devaluation of the peso, for example, caused a dramatic drop in numbers of tourists visiting Caye Caulker because they found better bargains for their dollar in Mexico. In spite of these problems, there are measures that can be taken to have as much local control of the tourist business as possible.

On Caye Caulker, foreign investment in tourist facilities has been discouraged, with islanders maintaining ownership of land and controlling investment in improvements on the land. In contrast, nearby San Pedro and Caye Chapel, both of whom can accomodate tourists arriving by air, have developed almost entirely through foreign money. One islander commented:

> On Caye Caulker we saw what happened on San Pedro. It used to be for the San Pedranos, but now all the development is by foreigners and the profit goes to them. We want to develop Caye Caulker ourselves. When we can get loans like $100,000 to $200,000 then we will develop ourselves, but until then we are holding on to our own land. We don't sell to foreigners. On San Pedro, the people all live on the back street. We keep the front for ourselves. Mr. Marsh, he's selling land to foreigners, but it's back land and it's not in the village. At the moment, I still make more by hauling traps, but if I expand my hotel in Belize City where the tourist trade is

> constant, I could make more than I do here on
> a hotel. Here the tourism is seasonal and you
> make more if you do lobster all the season.

The few foreign investments begun on the island have failed in part because of the lack of cooperation from local people. Several foreign investors have tried to get a foothold on Caye Caulker. 'Eden Isles', a resort at the southern tip of the island, and a scuba diving group that owns land near the cut, have both had serious problems. In the late 1970's Eden Isles was ransacked and stripped clean when its managers were arrested for cocaine smuggling. It has never opened again. The thatched cottages built at the cut to house large groups of divers were once burned to the ground, and although they have been rebuilt, the capital investment in the property is now very limited. Following their preference for noninterference, the islanders as a group have not taken measures to ensure that foreign investments be protected from acts of vandalism. Furthermore, for reasons that are none too clear, the airstrip on the island has never been completed thus limiting the numbers and kinds of tourists likely to make their way to Caye Caulker.

An important point is that the islanders have limited their investments to the use of cash rebates from the co-op rather than relying on credit from a bank. When they do need credit, for example, for fishing equipment, they can borrow from the co-op. In general they do not need to become indebited to banks, either national or foreign. Secondly their investments in tourism are modest expansions of existing facilities using family members as partners in the work of running a hotel, restaurant or shop. They have not built expensive, luxury accomodations with high running costs. Finally, they have created a dual economy so that seasonal and annual fluxuations in one area are offset by a second source of income.

Recent Developments

Autonomy from exploitative foreign economies, local control of individual production and distribution, a balance between two sources of income, and compatibility with local ideals and organization are factors in the successful development of Caye Caulker. This development is successful not only because it has produced local wealth, but because it is culturally and socially constructive, building on cultural ideals and social relationships to achieve a measure of economic independence and political autonomy in a situation of national underdevelopment.

All of this development of course produced visible change on Caye Caulker. Since first visiting Caye Caulker in 1972, I have witnessed virtually the entire development of tourism on the island. The increased contact with the outside, both through economic ties developed by the cooperative as well as through the influx of tourists to the island, has had a marked effect on Caye Caulker. The most obvious effect is the change in technology and products from industrial countries, both in the form of basic services such as plumbing and electricity, and consumer goods such as washing machines and televisions.

During the seventies Caye Caulker obtained constant electrical current, the telephone, and indoor plumbing with septic tanks. Though the Village Council had acquired a used electrical generator in 1957, the current was neither constant nor reliable. It broke down often and the voltage fluctuated wildly. Electrical appliances had a short life span under these conditions. Today the island still relies on used generators, there are two backup generators in case one fails, and the generating plant is staffed round-the- clock by three employees who work eight-hour shifts. With electrical current constant and more reliable, it became possible to run electrical appliances such as washing machines, refrigerators and freezers. This eliminated the need for many of the traditional types of food preservation and allowed for much needed food storage.

The first telephone connected Caye Caulker with the mainland in 1973. Today there is still one main exchange for the island, but as many as twenty-five families have telephone extensions in their homes. They use them to keep in touch with nuclear family members who work or attend school in Belize City. Some families which are divided between Caye Caulker and the mainland phone one another daily to keep up with news. In addition the common use of motorized skiffs makes it possible for families on Caye Caulker to have easier contact with families and institutions on the mainland. Some families with high school age children in Belize City can virtually commute from their fishing business on Caye Caulker to a home in Belize City. Motors also allow a more constant flow of outsiders to the island.

During the seventies, the first vehicle appeared on the island. A small tractor was transported to the island by an American who used it to haul cargo. There are now three jeeps on the caye for that purpose, along with a few bicycles, a three-wheeler, and two scooters, whose owners ride them around and around the village for entertainment in the evenings.

In 1972 the islanders had no plumbing. They drew water with a bucket from a well near the house and used outhouses at the end of the pier. Now outhouses have been replaced with indoor plumbing, electric water pumps and septic tanks. Although a few outhouses are still in use, a recent government edict allows no construction of new outhouses. Partly these changes are a response to the needs of tourists, but they also have been encouraged by the government because of the subsequent threat of hepatitis the tourists have brought with them. The introduction of septic tanks has reduced the risk of communicable diseases, particularly for children who swim off the shore, but it may pose a future threat to the purity of well water. The introduction of indoor plumbing has also brought about the demise of early morning socializing at the outhouses on the piers.

In 1982 television reception became clear enough to be viewable. Most families immediately got television sets, and now many islanders spend their evenings watching American television programs on the Chicago station they receive. They get their daily dose of American civilization with exercise programs in the morning and "The Jeffersons' every night at 7:00. Whereas whole families used to go down to their pier to cool off in the evenings, many of them now gather together in the living room to watch TV. On the other hand, they now have a source of news other than the government controlled Radio Belize even though they have to watch Belikan Beer commercials along with it.

Many of these innovations have diminished Caye Caulker's isolation, bringing it into closer contact with mainland Belize and the rest of the world. At the same time they tend to decrease interdependence between nuclear families. However, because most of these changes have taken place only in the last few years, it is too soon to observe any substantial cultural impact.

The most important change in the last decade is undoubtedly the result of an increasingly cash-oriented economy, bolstered by high lobster prices, and the growth of tourism. During the 1978-79 lobster season, lobster prices increased dramatically, elevating Caye Caulker fishermen into affluence. Although incomes had been growing steadily since the establishment of the co-op, this sudden jump in prices and the continued high production have combined to make Caye Caulker one of the most affluent villages in Central America. Within the span of two decades Caye Caulker developed from a poor village, dependent on subsistence fishing, meagre cocal incomes, and the generosity of kin and neighbors, to a relatively wealthy village where people work for themselves and individual families are increasingly self-sufficient. One woman who has two brothers on the caye, explained that they don't visit one another or exchange help as often as they used to because "We don't need to. We all have the same amount. We all have enough. But when I was sick before Christmas, then they came to visit and offer help."

In general, formal cash agreements are beginning to replace informal exchanges of goods and services. A few people now hire young men or women to work in their restaurants or hotels. This innovation of wage labor in the tourist industry is related to the increasing cash-orientation of the islanders and the island economy in general.

> I used to be able to bum a ride into Belize.
> If someone was going in, he would take me with
> him. But now if I want to go, I have to pay
> for it. Same sort of thing, it used to be
> that if a guy had a big catch, I'd help him
> with the catch and he'd give me some fish in
> return. Now I have to pay him for the fish
> and he pays someone to help him with the
> catch.

As a result of the success of its fishing industry, the growth of tourism, and population pressure on its scarce land resources, Caye Caulker has also experienced some demographic changes in recent years. According to an unofficial 1980 census, Caye Caulker has a population of 413 people. During the peak of the tourist season there may also be as many as 300 tourists on the island. Geographically the island has expanded to two new locations. A settlement of foreigners has sprung up at the south end of the village in an area known locally as 'the bush'. The dense underbrush and accompanying mosquitoes and sandflies in the area prevented many islanders from settling there. The settlement has become known as Marcialtown after Marcial Alamina, who acquired the whole section of land at the back of the island in about 1937 and sold it to individual foreigners in the 1970's. Several houses have been constructed, and a few more are in progress. They are owned primarily by Americans and Canadians in their late twenties or thirties who work in the north during the summer and spend their winters on Caye Caulker.

Beyond the north end of the village, the 'New Site' is developing near the Cut. Land in the village, in traditional family localities, has become scarce. Large plots of family-owned land have already been subdivided among children as much as is possible, and few families are willing to sell any extra land to non-family. As a case in point, the land that belonged to old Mr. Lenos and has been passed down in his family has now been divided as much as is possible among three relatives and two tourist businesses, and his great-great-grandsons have had to obtain land through the government raffle at the Cut. To accommodate the islanders' need for more land the Belizean government has authorized distribution of land north of the village by lottery. A result of the lottery system, is that the community at the New Site is developing in a very different pattern from the kin localities of the old village. However, there are already indications that clusters of kin are beginning to form at the 'new site.'

The island's demography has changed not only in terms of distribution, but also in terms of ethnic homogeneity. The original population was almost completely Mestizo. However, the prospects for fishing have attracted several Creole and Carib fishermen to Caye Caulker. A few Central Americans, from El Salvador, Guatemala, and Honduras have also settled on Caye Caulker. As the number of foreigners visiting the island grew throughout the seventies, some of them have stayed, and many of them make Caye Caulker their second home. Growing tourism has also attracted 'Rastafarians' from Belize City, known locally as "the boys from Belize". Partly because of the influx of Belizeans and foreigners, and the increase in crimes, since 1983 fences have been erected around homes and hotels, cutting up the open spaces on the island and restricting the flow of outsiders into people's yards.

Another result of the influx of foreigners and Belizeans is the increasingly more visable drug use on the island. The marijuana trade on the mainland of Belize has been growing rapidly mainly because the profits are so huge. In the Northern part of the country, milpa farming has turned to marijuana production and planes land daily to load, and transport the drug to the U.S. market. Select areas in Belize have also been stopping places for cocaine traffic. However on Caye Caulker, although marijuana use is not unusual, the islanders generally prefer rum and, for the most part, do not make a living from the marijuana trade. The local dealers are primarily nonislanders or young islanders who do not have the large incomes obtainable from fishing or tourism.

Tourism has also opened up economic opportunities for women. In response to tourist needs women sell take-away food from their homes, serve meals in their homes or cook meals for a designated eating place. They squeeze oranges, papayas and limes and sell the juice in old rum bottles from their houses. They also work along with their husbands in the daily business of running a hotel. All of these sources of income are new for women and have given women work that is compatible with their roles as housewife, cook and mother. Most important, this is work that they can do on the island as members of their extended families. They do not have to live in Belize City or abroad to work. The possibility of earning a good income releases women from total economic dependence on a father or husband.

Although Caye Caulker is still characterized by the features that have shaped it historically; a strong sense of individualism and autonomy, egalitarian forms of organization, fishing as the primary mode of production, and the family as the focus of individual loyalty, with the advent of the cooperative, tourism, motorized skiffs, mass communication and an increasing affluence, the days of isolation for Caye Caulker are over. The traditional ideals of noninterference and autonomy discourage cooperation and community action. As Caye Caulker has increasing contact with the outside, these ideals will be tested for their viability both for individuals, as well as for the future of the island.

VIII

Conclusions

The development of Caye Caulker is the story of the interrelationship between the individual, the wider network of kin to which the individual is connected, and an economic system that promotes individual entrepreneurs. Caye Caulker functions not as a community, but as a collection of individuals with links to a number of groups that range from the local household to international business. Although the focus of this book is on these interrelationships, the individual is the primary unit on Caye Caulker making direct links with all other units.

In its early years, Caye Caulker developed in much the same way as any area under a colonial government. A few entrepreneurs working with colonial export companies began to extract raw materials from the island. Beginning with coconut plantations, they later moved to lobster production with islanders acting as workers in the system. The colonial model of exploitation was established. Raw products were produced for foreign companies who obtained export agreements and quotas from a colonial government. In return manufactured goods were sold to the islanders (see Figure IV).

Figure IV. Model of Colonial Exploitation on Caye
        Caulker

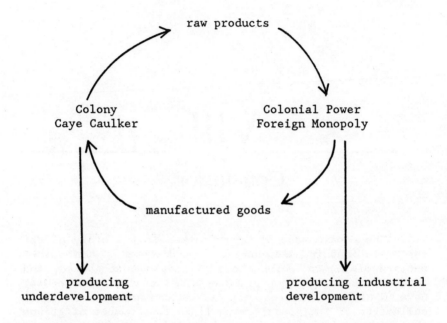

raw products

Colony
Caye Caulker

Colonial Power
Foreign Monopoly

manufactured goods

producing
underdevelopment

producing industrial
development

    This classic colonial situation found in both the
Caribbean and in Latin America contained certain
differences on Caye Caulker. Caye Caulker had no
indigenous population nor were slaves brought in as
workers. The island was populated in the late 1840's by
Mestizos from Yucatan who came to the island after fleeing
the caste wars there. A plantation system with slavery,
and later a strict race/class hierarchy, did not develop.
Ruling families did not take root. Furthermore the area
remained in isolation from the Colonial government.
    The Mestizo population brought with them a kinship
structure based on strong family ties. The original
families on the island developed wider networks of kin
concentrated into kin localities. This network of kin
functions as a cooperative unit, with the individual
fulfilling certain obligations and receiving in return
certain kinds of support (Figure V).

Figure V. Model of Cooperative Relationship between the
Individual and the Kin Group

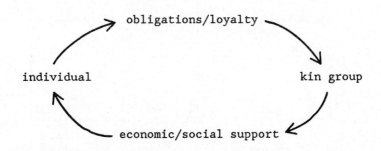

Reciprocal exchanges of goods and services between kin
have the important effect of helping the individual to
achieve economic independence.

Social interaction and organization beyond the
kinship network are based on the ideals of individual
autonomy and egalitarianism. Islanders believe that
individuals have the right to determine their own
behavior, without outside interference, even from family
members. While these ideals can function in casual
interactions, they have been an obstacle to the formation
of larger organizations. Thus in order for an
organization to succeed on Caye Caulker, it must interfere
as little as possible with the ideals of individual
autonomy and egalitarianism, and it must meet a recognized
need. Any organization which islanders perceive as
authoritarian or unnecessary has little chance of success.
Wider forms of social organization on Caye Caulker are
conspicuously lacking, and it is in this sense that the
island is more a collection of individuals rather than a
community.

In this context, the islanders created, during a
period of economic hardship and dissatisfaction with the
colonial model of exploitation, a fishing cooperative that
has dramatically changed their economic situation. The
structure and function of the cooperative parallels that
of the kinship network shown in Figure V. Basically the
co-op mediates between individual islanders and buyers
from the international market (see Figure VI).

Figure VI. Model of Relationship of Producer, Co-op and
International Buyer

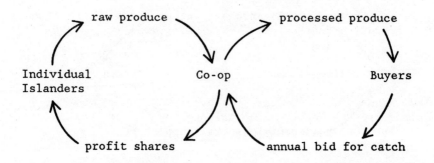

This arrangement has allowed Caye Caulker fishermen to obtain a better price for their produce, to exert greater control over its distribution and at the same time to maintain their traditional ideals. Furthermore, the co-op has been managed with an eye to its independence as an organization. Islanders have insisted on managing the co-op themselves and have not handed over decision-making power to government authorities, international banks, or hired professional managers. The compatibility of the ideals and structure of the co-op with the ideals and structure of island social organization is a key to its success.

Finally Caye Caulker has continued to expand its economic base by developing tourism. Profits from fishing have been invested in tourist-related businesses, and these investments produce a direct return to the individual islander. (See Figure VII.)

Figure VII. Model of Relationship of Islander to Tourist
Business and Tourists

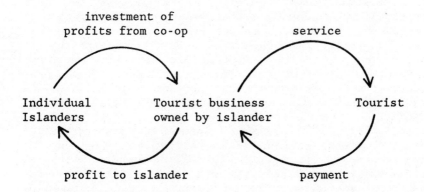

Women have also been incorporated into the tourist
business, thereby creating a new category of producers
within the traditional family structure.

As islanders have come increasingly into contact
with the world outside, their reaction has been to protect
their resources from other Belizeans and foreigners, by
moving in the direction of individual self-advancement
rather than community development. Extended families have
become more commercially oriented with less and less
interaction based on reciprocity. Yet the islanders have
kept control of the tourist development on the island and
have avoided foreign investments in much the same way that
they control the co-op and have avoided foreign domination
of lobster production and distribution. Furthermore,
tourists have been accommodated into island social life
relatively easily because of the island ideals of
tolerance and noninterference with others. Yet there are
signs that increased tourism is creating new pressures on
the community in the form of a greater frequency of theft,
drug use and personal assault. Unless the islanders
develop new strategies to deal with these problems in
their autonomous fashion, they face the possibility of
government intervention.

For the first time in over 30 years Belize has a new
government led by the UDP (United Democratic Party). The
UDP is composed of young, relatively inexperienced
politicians who are mainly pro-U.S. in orientation. There
are already signs that the government will be encouraging

private American investment in the country and receiving more American government aid than ever before. A locally controlled cooperative and a reluctance to allow foreign investment on Caye Caulker may not receive favorable treatment by a government that wants to encourage foreign investment. Instead they may promote areas such as San Pedro. San Pedro has developed primarily through foreign investment and in 1984 became a township, indicating its interest in forming closer alliances with the administrative structure of the national government. With the increasing strategic importance of Belize in the Central American-Caribbean region, the U.S. will be trying to consolidate its interests in one of the democratically-elected, stable governments in the region. Caye Caulker represents a successful local development through individual entrepreneurship and cooperation with each other as producers. The cooperative method employed on Caye Caulker does not favor the international buyer who has to pay a high price for Caye Caulker produce. The Caye Caulker approach has, instead, favored the islanders themselves who are reaping the financial benefits of their labor, both in fishing and in tourism. Caye Caulker is a model of local development that successfully benefits the local producers, but the islanders will have to maintain vigilance in their broader political relationships to continue their independence.

Bibliography

Acheson, James, Fishing, Ann. Rev. Anthropol., 1981, 10:275-316.

Ashcraft, Norman, "Some Aspects of Domestic Organization in British Honduras" in The Family in the Caribbean, Stanford N. Gerber, ed., University of Puerto Rico: Institute of Caribbean Studies, 1968.

Ashcraft, Norman, Colonialism and Underdevelopment: Processes of Political Economic Change in British Honduras, New York: Teachers College Press,Teachers College, Columbia University, 1973.

Barry, Tom, Beth Wood and Deb Preusch, Dollars and Dictators, A Guide to Central America, Albuquerque, New Mexico: The Resource Center, 1982.

Bolland, O. Nigel, The Formation of a Colonial Society, Johns Hopkins University Press, 1977.

Bradley, Leo, "Glimpses of our History", Belize City: National Collection, Bliss Institute, October 1962, Vol. 4A.

Craig, Alan K., Geography of Fishing in British Honduras and Adjacent Coastal Areas, Baton Rouge, Louisiana: Coastal Studies Institute, Louisiana State University, 1966.

Cross, Malcolm, Urbanization and Urban Growth in the Caribbean, Cambridge: Cambridge University Press, 1979.

Dippel, John, "Looking for the Last Maine Lobster", Oceans, Jan./Feb., Vol. 13, no. 1, 1980, pages 61-63.

Dobson, Narda, A History of Belize, Port of Spain, Trinidad and Tobago: Longman Caribbean, 1973.

Escure, Genevieve, "Contrastive Patterns of Intragroup and Intergroup Interaction in the Creole Continuum of Belize", Language in Society, II, 1982, pages 239-264.

Forman, Shepard, The Raft Fishermen, Tradition and Change in the Brazilian Peasant Economy, Bloomington: Indiana University Press, 1970.

Godfrey, Glenn D., _Ambergris Caye: Paradise with a Past_, Belize, a Central American: Cubola Productions, 1983.

Gonzalez, Nancy Solien, "Household and Family in the Caribbean: Some Definitions and Concepts" in _The Black Woman Cross-Culturally_, Filomina Chioma Steady, ed. Cambridge, Mass.: Schenkman Publishing Co., 1981, pages 421-429.

Gordon, Edmund, _Phases of Development and Underdevelopment in a Caribbean Fishing Village: San Pedro, Belize_, Ph.D. dissertation, Stanford University, 1981.

Gregory, James R., "Cooperatives: Failures Versus Successes", _Belizean Studies_, Vol. 12, No. 5, 1984.

Kerns, Virginia, _Women and the Ancestors_, University of Illinois Press, 1983.

Kottak, Conrad Phillip, _Assault on Paradise, Social Change in a Brazilian Village_, New York: Random House, 1983.

Lewis, Gordon K., _The Growth of the Modern West Indies_, New York: Monthly Review Press, 1968.

Lewis, Gordon K., _Main Current in Caribbean Thought_, Baltimore, MD: John Hopkins University Press, 1983.

Lewis, Oscar, _The Children of Sanchez_, Vintage Books, 1963.

Martinez-Alier, Verena, _Marriage, Class and Color in Nineteenth Century Cuba, A Study of Racial Attitudes and Sexual Values in a Slave Society_, London: Cambridge University Press, 1974.

1981 World Bank Atlas, Washington, D.C.: The World Bank, 1982.

The Northern Fishermen Cooperative Annual Report, 1982, 1983, 1984.

149

Population Census of the Commonwealth Caribbean, 1970. University of the West Indies, Census Research Programme.

Reams, Joanne Reppert, ed., Background Notes, Belize, Washington, D.C.: U.S. Department of State, 1982.

Reed, Nelson, The Caste War of Yucatan, Stanford: Stanford University Press, 1964.

Setzekorn, William, Formerly British Honduras: A Profile of the New Nation of Belize, Newark, California: Dumbarton Press, 1975.

Smith, Raymond T., "The Family and the Modern World System: Some Observations from the Caribbean", Journal of Family History, Vol. 3, No. 4, Winter, 1978, pages 337-359.

Spradley, James, Participant Observation, Holt, Rinehart and Winston, 1980.

Spradley, James, The Ethnographic Interview, Holt, Rinehart and Winston, 1979.

Sutherland, Anne and Kroshus, Laurie, "A Social History of Caye Caulker", Belizean Studies, Vol. 13, No. 1, 1985.

Sutherland, Anne, "Kinship and Family Structure on Caye Caulker", Belizean Studies, Vol. 13, Nos. 5 & 6, 1985.

Sutton, Constance and Makiesky-Barrow, Susan, "Social Inequality and Sexual Status in Barbados" in The Black Woman Cross-Culturally, Filomina Chioma Steady, ed., Cambridge, Mass.: Schenkman Publishing Co., 1981, pages 469-498.

van den Bor, Wout, Island Adrift: The Social Organization of a Small Caribbean Community. The Case of St. Eustatius. Luden: Department of Caribbean Studies, Royal Institute of Linguistics and Anthropology, 1981.

Vega, Susanna, "The Development of Spiney Lobster Fishing in Belize, 1920-1977," Belizean Studies, Vol. 7, No. 2, March, 1979, pages 1-6.

Index